Semi-States in Crisis

The Challenge for Industrial Relations in the ESB and Other Major Semi-State Companies

Tim Hastings

Oak Tree Press

Dublin

in association with
Graduate School of Business
University College Dublin

Oak Tree Press
4 Arran Quay, Dublin 7
a division of Cork Publishing Limited

© 1994 Timothy M. Hastings

A catalogue record of this book is
available from the British Library.

ISBN 1-872853-79-X (pbk.)
ISBN 1-872853-80-3 (hbk.)

Printed in Ireland by Colour Books Ltd.

CONTENTS

PREFACE

The thesis on which this book is based, arose from a personal "hunch" that something momentous and unique was unfolding in the ESB during the shattering four day dispute in April 1991, which seriously reduced national power supplies. After sitting for several days and nights in the foyer of Jury's Hotel in Dublin, covering the strike as Industrial Correspondent for Independent Newspapers, the demeanour and approach of both sides to the row suggested that more than the standard industrial relations issues were involved.

The handling of the strike by both sides implied that something close to a crisis of the bargaining system itself was underway when over 7,000 staff went out in support of the electricians' call. The normal internal safety nets had fallen away to reveal a row about money, but more fundamentally about a huge frustration which had been building up for the previous ten years. Informal channels of communication had either broken down or not existed, and management appeared to be paralysed by the enormity of the dispute and the public backlash it created. And when the dispute, the worst in the ESB since the 1960s was resolved, the Government, senior politicians and civil servants seemed determined that the conditions which had led to the strike should never arise again.

The key to the dispute and its long term implications was its timing; it broke just as an alternative personnel strategy was being tried in generation, the side of the company facing the greatest change. It also occurred as management disillusionment with the ability of the bargaining system to deliver change reached its peak. Most significantly of all, it happened just as the Board was considering the implications of the new EU proposals for deregulation of the European electricity industry. The force, impact and reaction to the 1991 dispute and the depth of problems it unearthed, produced transformation conditions in ESB industrial relations. The strike acted as catalyst for major change, which it ultimately accelerated. The latest instalment of this new cost cutting agenda emerged in early October this year in the McKinsey proposals to cut numbers in the company by 2,900 and introduce major changes in work practices, particularly in generation, where staffing levels are being halved. This poses a major challenge to the new relationship of trust and partnership fostered by both sides since the 1991 dispute.

Developments in a number of other state companies since the 1991 strike, particularly in 1994, suggested that the sort of change and trauma that emerged in the ESB was surfacing elsewhere. The major disputes in TEAM Aer Lingus and in Irish Steel in summer 1994 provided examples of state companies, whose bargaining agendas had major difficulty coming to terms with the sort of global competition now facing both the private and public sectors. In view of these developments, it was decided that the book should be expanded to include an analysis and description of the major developments in these companies and of similar disputes in RTE, Irish Rail, Aer Lingus and An Post. All these rows represent the face of the new demands being made on the Irish semi-state sector, parts of which up to now have been shielded from such demanding levels of change, in some instances because of their social mandate. The ESB represents a case study of a company where many of the demands that have been tabled separately in other semi-state companies are being sought simultaneously.

I would firstly like to thank Professor Bill Roche of the Graduate School of Business, University College Dublin, for his highly committed supervision of my original Master of Commerce thesis "Crisis and Transformation in ESB Industrial Relations". His concerned, but ultimately challenging approach made me feel privileged to work with someone who had such a total grasp of developments in industrial relations at both a theoretical and practical level.

Secondly I would like to thank my wife, Carmel Traynor, for her support and encouragement and Independent Newspapers, my employers, for their help and assistance, particularly Editor Vincent Doyle, Paul Dunne and David Halloran.

Major thanks are also due to the ESB for their openness throughout the entire research process and for their ultimate agreement that the academic material could be used in book form. In particular I would like to thank the Director of Personnel, Lorcan Canning for his permission to examine the ESB Files Registry and the Corporate Communications Manager Larry Donald, for his patience with the final checking of details.

I would also like to thank Paul Sweeney of SIPTU for help with the job figures on other semi-states and his views on recent developments and Brian Sheehan, editor of *Industrial Relations News*

(IRN), for advice and suggestions on the final script. Thanks are also due to Frank Traynor, for assistance with tables, Linda Doyle of the Department of Industrial Relations in UCD and David Givens of Oak Tree Press.

Most of all, however, I would like to record my appreciation for the time and insight provided by various managers, union officials and others in ESB and elsewhere who helped and whose identity must remain confidential. I would also like to thank some other senior personnel and union figures for their comments on suggestions on the final script. Ultimately, the responsibility for any mistakes of interpretation or fact rests with the author.

Tim Hastings
November 1994

LIST OF ABBREVIATIONS

ATGWU	Amalgamated Transport and General Workers' Union
CCR	The Cost and Competitiveness Review in ESB
CIE	Coras Iompair Éireann
CWU	The Communications Workers' Union
ESB	Electricity Supply Board
ESBOA	Electricity Supply Board Officers' Assocation
HRM	Human Resource Management
IALPA	Irish Airline Pilots' Association
IBEC	Irish Business and Employers' Confederation
ICTU	Irish Congress of Trade Unions
IPPs	Independent Power Producers
IR	Industrial Relations
IRN	Industrial Relations News
JIC	Joint Industrial Council
LRC	Labour Relations Commission
NBRU	The National Bus and Railworkers' Union
NGP	New Generation Programme
NUJ	National Union of Journalists
RTE	Radio Telefís Éireann
SIPTU	Services Industrial Professional and Technical Union
SPI	Station Performance Incentive
TEAM	The Experts in Aircraft Maintenance
TEEU	The Technical Engineering and Electrical Union
TPA	Third Party Access
PESP	Programme for Economic and Social Progress
PCW	Programme for Competitiveness and Work

Chapter One

SEMI-STATES IN CRISIS

Introduction

Irish commercial semi-state companies are undergoing unprecedented levels of change. Their markets are under threat from new and more aggressive low cost operators; their economic justification is being challenged and the regulatory environment within which they operate is being dictated by European rather than purely national considerations. Their commercial mandate is being redefined by a variety of forces which are in the main external and are far removed from traditional domestic political control under which they were formerly shielded.

Developments within the Electricity Supply Board (ESB) provide an example of a semi-state company confronting just such change and whose collective bargaining system, up to very recently, has had severe difficulty coping with the challenges it faces. The four day 1991 electricians' dispute exposed major weaknesses in the Board's industrial relations, including weaknesses of bargaining at workplace level, lack of informal relations and a management that had lost faith in its own internal procedures and failed to anticipate the strike. The momentous dispute resulted in almost two-thirds of the Board's 10,000 staff staying out of work for the best part of a week in late April 1991 in support of an action launched by the electricians' union, the Technical Engineering and Electrical Union (TEEU). Despite having less than 150 members within the key generation area, the electricians' strike received devastating levels of support from other groups right across the company and had a huge impact, principally because of the "unfinished business" with the main categories of staff and management style. The strike resulted in thousands of workers being laid off in the wider industrial sector due to lack of power supplies. The outcry by a largely unprepared public against the action was unprecedented. This forced a major political reassessment of the role and structure of the Board. Many at a senior political level saw the ESB as a "state within a state" and felt that such an action should never be allowed happen again.

The fall-out, internally and externally, from the 1991 dispute was to have a lasting impact on the company's industrial relations culture, forcing a major reassessment on all sides. Evidence of the new style of relationship, some of it influenced by human resource management thinking, emerged in the unions' calm and reasoned reaction to the McKinsey proposals, published in September 1994, for job reductions of 2,900 and huge work practice changes. Human resource management thinking, as will be discussed in the next chapter, is a new approach which emphasises the creation of shared values and aims between management and staff geared to a changing and increasingly global marketplace. It downplays the notion of conflict based on traditional collective bargaining models.

The implications of the 1991 strike for internal ESB relations will be considered later in greater detail in the context of the questions it posed about the traditional methods of conflict resolution in the Board and the new ground breaking approaches it eventually gave way to. These will be explored in the final chapters after an examination of more recent developments.

The logic of state companies providing a social service — which buttressed much of their development, their consensual management style and fairly conservative internal thinking — is undergoing a major reassessment. On top of this, a political agenda which believes that much of the State sector would be more efficient and more productive in private hands has gained a standing in the body politic that would have been unthinkable a few years ago. The rapid pace of change in semi-state companies has led many observers to suggest that by the end of the decade all that will distinguish semi-state companies from their private sector counterparts is ownership; their styles of management and industrial relations may have converged, but in reality this is likely to be less than total because of the political factor. Both sectors will by then, some argue, be subject to equal commercial and market pressures. In this climate, poor performance and weak management is less likely to be tolerated by a Government which supports the injection of private sector performance criteria into the wider public sector and commercial semi-states.

Aer Lingus, Irish Steel, Irish Rail and TEAM are just the latest firms to undergo crises of major proportions where their future is threatened by a combination of high costs and severe losses, rapidly changing international markets and an industrial relations culture which has had difficulty adapting to the new market-orientated pressures. Like the other major disputes before them in

RTE and An Post, the difficulties in each company gave expression to particular types of industrial relations traditions which were under severe pressure and which formed the public face of the crises in these firms. Each crisis was handled differently by management and unions, suggesting varying levels of preparedness for the new realities. The common thread running through each dispute is a management-driven agenda for change and rationalisation, rather than the traditional collective bargaining issues of pay and conditions. Cost reduction, through the introduction of new work practices and job reduction, was the objective in tandem with a new focus on actual customer needs.

By late 1994 the Irish semi-state sector is facing into the sort of the change and rationalisation programmes that were the hallmark of many private sector disputes in the 1980s. Difficulties in firms like Ford, Packard Electric, Semperit and latterly Waterford Glass made these companies household names, as they sought to adjust to international trading conditions with painful implications for their workforces both in terms of work practices and pay. Major job shedding and restructuring programmes have already been completed in Aer Lingus and Irish Steel and are about to get underway at Telecom Éireann and the ESB. These changes pose as many challenges for managers as they do for unions and demand particular leadership roles on either side which have not been called for in the past.

The pace of change and the changing public perception of semi-states has been so rapid that some trade union officials and Government ministers now privately distinguish between the companies that have "crossed the Rubicon" to new management thinking and a more responsive trade union and company culture. As particular semi-states head into, or emerge from, their separate crises, the tradition of chief executives being appointed from within the organisation is being dispensed with. Layers of management, and in some cases chief executives, are being forced to resign before or immediately after the crisis. And a range of new outside appointments is being made to State firms at private sector salaries, effectively dispensing with the Government's traditional pay restrictions.

All these developments have major implications for the type and resilience of industrial relations policies pursued by these organisations. They represent a threat to the monopoly culture that dominated not only management thinking but formed part of the overall trade union outlook within them. They also pose a major challenge to the traditional orthodoxy of industrial relations within State firms. In some cases, but by no means all, this found expression in an approach that was inward looking, craft-orientated and heavily proceduralised. Some of this thinking was underpinned by what many have called the "jobs for life" culture of the semi-states, in which the relations with the State itself, rather than the customer, were seen as the vital ingredient.

Job-shedding, demands for dropping or modifying sometimes antiquated work practices, and severe cost reduction programmes have been the hallmarks of these public sector modernisation programmes. In the case of the ESB and RTE, strikes became part of the change process to a greater or lesser extent, while in other companies such as Aer Lingus the more exposed industrial relations culture proved capable of handling the change agenda without recourse to stoppages. In TEAM, the very way the company was set up as a subsidiary of Aer Lingus, its style of management and union leadership, contributed to the severe inability to adjust to work practice and cost reduction changes until the firm was placed in examinership.

These demands reflect a fairly rapid change in the country's national industrial relations agenda with pay issues effectively catered for by centralised national agreements like the Programme for Economic and Social Progress (PESP) and more recently the Programme for Competitiveness and Work (PCW) signed in early 1994. Employers' demands for pay cuts or freezes, resulting from increased global competition, have surfaced on the industrial relations agenda as never before and it was only a matter of time before similar demands appeared in the semi-state companies. As Ray McGee, the Director of Conciliation at the Labour Relations Commission, noted recently:

> Time was when we had national agreements, an awful lot of cases that were dealt with rigidly under their provisions and people could or could not pay their basic terms. You could fix them in half an hour or be in the Labour Court in fifteen minutes. Now a more business-driven or employer-driven agenda operates, embracing international competition, the need for downsizing, competitiveness and World Class Manufacturing (*Business and Finance*, 16 June 1994).

Since the 1990s in particular, State policy towards semi-state companies has undergone a major alteration with the advent of the Culliton Report (*Report of the Industrial Policy Review Group*,

January 1992) and the Moriarty Report (*Employment Through Enterprise — The Response of the Government to the Moriarty Task Force on the Implementation of the Cullliton Report*, May 1993) — which emphasised the role of State firms as facilitators. These reports' major concern was with the prices charged and the level of service provided to the wider economy by State firms and their impact on the input costs to industry. The approach they outlined sought to reinvigorate the role of the State sector and separate it out from the "heavy hand" of Government itself, which was seen as a brake on the development of an enterprise culture in the public domain. The parameters of this new approach to semi-state companies are just emerging. The shifting mandate for commercial semi-states was outlined in early 1994, at the time of the signing of the PCW by the Minister for Transport, Energy and Communications Brian Cowen. He noted:

> Given the historical operating environment of many of our semi-state companies, one in which there has been no exposure to the competitive need for responsiveness to the market, a fundamental shift in the style of their operation is called for. What was considered appropriate in the past is no longer acceptable to the recipients of State services and to me (Dáil Éireann report, 4 March 1994).

Speaking in the same debate the Minister noted that "it seems a pity that it is only when a serious critical and imminent challenge has to be faced that semi-state bodies have demonstrated the ability to react". Such crisis management may have helped in the past but in an increasingly competitive era, this approach carried within it the seeds of potential disaster. The Minister's comments before the crisis in TEAM Aer Lingus were prophetic.

At a management level, the tried and trusted approach to the running of State firms which emphasises accountability above all is being seriously questioned. New demands are being made of executives in semi-state companies. In the industrial relations arena, a new management approach which confronts embedded practices is emerging which is less passive in the face of union power. Private sector values are being infused into State firms by chief executives, or consultants, whose outlook and strategic vision differ greatly from those whose careers were built within the organisation.

In parallel, the role of the State as shareholder in semi-state companies is being redefined from the more active interventionist

approach to a policy of setting a tougher and more commercially
defined mandate within which the firms as departmental satellites must operate. Emerging European deregulation is likely to
redefine rather than suppress totally the sort of political intervention that has only been a feature of Irish state companies. The
nature of the intervention is likely to change. With many of the
structural alterations in semi-states requiring changes in the
companies founding acts, like the 1927 Electricity (Supply) Act,
the formal legal and political framework within which some firms
operate is under review.

This chapter seeks to explore and analyse up-to-date developments in a number of semi-state companies. The forces creating a
climate for change, and in some cases crisis, will be examined under a number of headings, including (a) new competitive and
commercial pressures; (b) the nature, type and rigidity or otherwise of the industrial relations practices within the companies and
their ability to adapt; and (c) the loosening of the political regulation and control and changes in political support. Management's
handling of its new remit and the implications for the hitherto
protected bargaining environments is also worthy of consideration.
The features of recent industrial relations upheavals in companies
such as Aer Lingus, RTE, An Post and Irish Steel will be examined after a brief outline of the disputes that catapulted them into
the headlines.

Developments within in the ESB, particularly since 1981 and
both during and after the 1991 dispute, which comprise the bulk of
this book, highlight the difficulty of winning change and responding both to price and competitive pressures in a highly structured
public sector bargaining environment. The case study of the ESB
reveals a management that became seriously disillusioned with its
own internal industrial relations machinery and a resulting
building up of pressure on both sides which ultimately found expression in the shattering 1991 strike and the "no give" policy
which led up to it. As the ESB's Director of Personnel Lorcan
Canning noted recently, "it is impossible to overstate the effect on
public and political opinion caused by that week of power cuts"
(Canning, 1994). Emphasising the seismic nature of the dispute,
Canning believed it had profoundly influenced public perception of
ESB and generated significant external pressure for change. He
added:

There was unprecedented public condemnation of ESB and everyone involved — management, unions and staff — and de-

mands for action by Government . . . there is little doubt that the electricians' strike was the catalyst which led Government at that particular time to embark on reviewing and restructuring the entire electricity supply industry in Ireland and to seriously consider breaking up the ESB.

The net effect of the dispute was to expose a management that had lost touch with feelings on the ground in its own company, partly through a communications gap at supervisory level. A more lasting impact was that the dispute undermined the confidence of top management in the ability of the standard bargaining processes to deliver change allowing a move towards a "soft" human resource management approach to take hold. The strike, and the public reaction to a week of power cuts, as well as apparent management impotence to immediately resolve it, led to the acceleration of a plan to divide the ESB into five separate business units. It ultimately played a significant part in a decision to instigate a major review of its cost base. Historical developments within ESB, political sanctioning of its internal bargaining machinery in the early 1970s followed by the turbulent strike-prone 1980s and the subsequent crisis, all provide us with a template to evaluate subsequent shifts in other companies.

What follows is an outline sketch of the history and background to the major disputes and crises in a number of key state companies in recent years. Developments in each company and how they will impact on the longer term structure of union management relations will be analysed later in the chapter in the context of the pointers outlined earlier.

Irish Steel

Irish Steel was created from the nationalisation of a private company which had gone into receivership in 1946. A modern steel mill was constructed in the late 1970s, but uncompetitive labour costs, a costly overhead structure and restructuring within the European steel industry coupled with deregulation presented major problems by the early 1990s. In the three years to 30 June 1994, total losses of £31 million were incurred, including redundancy costs the total figure is £35 million. In fact, according to the management plan published after a report was commissioned from a firm of accountants (Simpson Xavier Horwath, 1994), Irish Steel has lost £130 million since 1980 and the Government has invested £185 million, including bank guarantees, into the busi-

ness to maintain 560 jobs. This is the equivalent of £1 million a
month over that period. Irish Steel has not made a profit since
1989/90. In addition, in 1994 the Cobh-based semi-state traded in
a marketplace where there was a 50 per cent overcapacity for
some heavier steel items. The firm's peripheral geographical location was also a liability and pushed up transport costs. With labour costs accounting for 21 per cent of total costs, the newly appointed company executive chairman, Pat Dineen, in May 1994
demanded major changes.

Included were 151 redundancies; contracting out of services,
particularly non-core activities such as security; reductions of up
to 28 per cent in gross pay; elimination of restrictive practices to
attain a level of flexibility that equates with best world standards.
A target of reducing the cost base by £8.4 million was set, which
was to be matched by a further equity injection by the Exchequer,
subject to EU approval, of around £25 million.

Like the other disputes over rationalisation and survival considered here, Irish Steel proved to be particularly difficult to settle; no less than four interventions were required. A Labour Relations Commission peace bid was followed by an ICTU intervention
and then a Labour Court investigation. Ultimately, further ICTU
pressure for an aggregate ballot — after SIPTU members had accepted but craftworkers had rejected the outcome — was necessary. This only emerged after the board of the company, supported
by the Minister for Enterprise and Employment Ruairi Quinn,
threatened to liquidate the firm. After modifying the survival
plan, including removing the compulsory redundancy element for
the 200 staff who were to eventually leave, the Labour Court was
less than hopeful about Irish Steel's future:

> The business is losing some £12 million per annum and the
> savings estimated in the survival plan are in the region of £8
> million p.a. overall. In other words, the company will still not
> be viable in the normal commercial sense. Its longer term out-
> look depends on the achievement of new business and the es-
> tablishment of a partnership arrangement (LCR, 14506: 3).

The final element in the rescue emerged after 15 craftworkers
were suspended for refusing to change from a four to a three shift
system, following a return to work. After another ballot of craftsmen the rescue terms were eventually accepted. The breakthrough
came in late September when the 97 craft workers met and voted
by two to one to accept the Dineen plan, effectively reversing their

previous decision when they voted against by the same margin as part of the aggregate ballot. The dramatic final twist followed the Government decision to accept the advice of executive chairman Pat Dineen that it was not possible to save the company and that a liquidator be appointed. Later, following contact between the Tánaiste, Dick Spring, and the Bishop of Cloyne, John Magee, and the executive chairman, conditions were laid down for a return to work including acceptance from unions and workers in writing that they accepted the Dineen plan and that full severance pay would only be paid after 12 months on statutory severance entitlements. The unions said they could not comply with additional demands outside the Labour Court recommendation. But eventually a letter from each union confirming acceptance of the Dineen plan, together with signatures of all members, was considered adequate. The delay in full severance payments was reduced to six months after further ICTU intervention. This requirement was eventually dropped by the company in October 1994 in recognition of the commitment and co-operation given by the entire workforce.

An Post

Unions and management at An Post signed an historic agreement in September 1993 that allowed the introduction of computerised sorting and new work practices at a £15 million state-of-the-art sorting centre, the Dublin Mails Centre, off the Naas Road in West Dublin. The eventual transfer of letter handling to the new mails centre in early 1994 resulted in a number of weeks of late delivery that led to severe public criticism of An Post management. The breakthrough deal, which allowed the switch, was the climax to a process of negotiating a recovery plan that emerged after a six week disruptive dispute that began in late April 1992. This was sparked by a company plan to recruit 250 part-time and temporary staff in the Central Sorting Office in Dublin. In fact, company chief executive John Hynes had first tabled his "Viability Plan" in February 1991, six months after his appointment, when he was projecting losses of £16 million for that year. The plan included a move to the new computerised sorting centre, a single daily delivery, the use of roadside mailboxes, the closure of 550 sub post offices, 1,500 job cuts and major reductions in overtime. The radical blueprint, which was aimed at cutting costs, got a rough reception after Hynes declared that he would discuss how to implement it rather than the nuts and bolts of the blueprint itself. The hiring of part-time and temporary staff that ignited the row in Dublin was aimed at curbing the company's £21 million overtime bill — £12 million of which originated in Dublin. The focus was on a set of changes and alterations in work rules, some of which had a human resource management origin and which were aimed at creating greater flexibility and breaking down traditional rigidities. Management also argued that an earlier agreement, the 1987 "Partnership for Progress" deal had failed to generate savings and only served to push up costs.

But it turned out to be an unusual dispute in many ways. While technically in dispute with the company, David Begg, general secretary of the Communications Workers' Union, told his members employed in the Central Sorting Office to carry out their normal duties but not to work with the new recruits. He fought against internal pressure from some militant elements within his own union to launch normal all-out type industrial action at the Sheriff Street sorting office. In this he was stamping his control on the dispute, putting the onus on management to move and burying the history of unofficial action at the Central Sorting Office in Dublin which sparked the devastating 1979 national postal dispute. Management suspended 1,300 people in all, arguing that it had to hire temporary staff to reduce costs and avoid losses piling up.

A number of interesting side issues emerged during the dispute, principally management's inability to lay off staff because of the status of the majority of the pre-1984 employees as civil servants.

Behind the complex issues in the dispute, outside observers believed that underlying the row was a struggle "between a strong union seeking to 'trump' An Post's blueprint for change with its own agenda" (*Industrial Relations News* 22, 1992). Amid the political furore over the closure of the 550 sub post offices, consultants backed the company's original plans. This proposal was later turned down by the Government after a national campaign in which the Communications Workers' Union participated under the general banner of "Saving the Post Office," despite the fact that they did not represent the staff of the sub post offices. Effectively the issue provided them with a broadly populist banner to fight the company's overall cost reduction plans. At the end of the day the CWU won the creation of 80 permanent jobs out of the dispute but ended up facing job losses down the road as a result of the 1993 breakthrough agreement. But the final job loss total was less than half the original 1,500 projected figure in the original company plan. While the postal workers' union came out of the 1992 dispute looking stronger, the final Labour Relations Commission peace formula to end the six week old dispute gave the management some long-term gains. Acceptance of the formula tied the CWU into a process of change through negotiation and set a date of September 1992 for final adjudication for resolution that was far exceeded. While the CWU ended up conceding the principle of auxiliary or part-time staff in the Central Sorting Office — they had always operated in rural areas — the dispute was also about the union wanting to have a handle on change but more specifically handling it in its own way (*Business and Finance*, 4 June 1992). The dispute centred on efforts to bring in a range of changes and flexibilities, some of a human resource type, which presented a major challenge to the existing fairly rigid forms of working within the company.

RTE

Like the 1992 dispute in An Post, the RTE strike in early January of that year centred on a row over fundamental change in work practices in the State-funded broadcasting body. The row was more about local change than alterations arising from deregulation or intensified competition, and it demonstrated the poor state of industrial relations in the station. RTE management claimed that between 1984 and 1985 all its unions signed the agreement "Broadcasting for the 80s" which granted increases in excess of 20 per cent for ongoing changes arising out of the introduction of new technology. For their part, the unions and in particular SIPTU, the largest union at the station, claimed that significant changes over and above those included in this document had been conceded. Management saw any further concession of any on-going payment leading to a cycle of new pay claims.

Fifty members of SIPTU were taken off the payroll on Tuesday, 21 January, after negotiations on monetary compensation for a reduction in TV camera crews from three to two had failed to reach agreement the previous day. RTE refused to concede on-going payments and offered instead a lump sum of £1,000 in the form of £200 per year over five years. The suspensions followed a refusal by crews to work the new arrangements. The Labour Court in an earlier recommendation had largely backed the management's position. The changes had been deferred from the previous December at the request of SIPTU leader Bill Attley. The smaller

National Union of Journalists got involved when two of its members were suspended for operating the so-called internal disputes procedure under which they only took direction from designated executives during a dispute. Both SIPTU and the National Union of Journalists subsequently launched strike action. Government Ministers declined to appear on RTE's skeleton news service during the dispute which was maintained with the help of management grades.

The four week strike ended on Monday, 17 February 1992, when two of the three unions involved, SIPTU and the NUJ, accepted a Labour Court recommendation which proposed the establishment of a Special Adjudication Committee (SAC) to deal with issues relating to technological change and new work practices. Members of the other union involved, the TEEU, simply went back to work without formal acceptance. Under the agreement reached at the Labour Court, the lump sum compensation was increased to £1,750 for SIPTU members affected by the reduction in camera crew levels from three to two, and six upgradings were offered for sound and lighting staff. While about 70 per cent of the 1,300 SIPTU members accepted the recommendation, NUJ members voted by just 91 votes to 70 to return to work after one of the most bitter disputes in the station's history. Much of the NUJ anger was directed at their ten members who stayed at work. In fact, the substantive issue of the return to work occupied much of the time spent by both sides in the Labour Court. The NUJ wanted a non-victimisation clause and the Court insisted that any arrangements would have to be two-way and take into account the position of those who had stayed at work. The NUJ finally agreed that no action would be taken under its own disciplinary code against the ten management personnel in question, and management agreed that three management staff who agreed to support the strike, and who were subsequently demoted, would be restored to their original positions prior to the strike.

At one stage during the proceedings the unions put up a proposal for binding arbitration for six months on the core issue in the dispute but this was not accepted.

The Special Adjudication Committee was recommended by the Labour Court for the "specific and limited purpose of dealing with issues arising from technological change and changes in work practices and their consequences, including remuneration and compensation where appropriate" (LCR 13467). In the wake of the RTE dispute, ICTU assistant general secretary Kevin Duffy saw the succession stakes for the Director General post at the station and "one group of managers trying to outmanoeuvre another" as playing a part in delaying the ending the dispute. Part of the difficulty in finding a resolution was trying to get agreement between the managers in a multi-management structure in the station. Duffy added:

> This was a major factor in the dispute, the issues in any other set of circumstances could have been dealt with if there had been some sort of coherent management (*Business and Finance*, 25 June 1992).

Other figures close to the dispute on the management side later confirmed this view privately to the author. Management determination to use the dispute to lay down markers for the future was best summed up by the Director of Personnel, Christy Killeen, one week into the row:

> We are holding out for a resolution that will allow RTE to guarantee to the greatest extent possible the continuation of public service broadcasting and not have short term solutions (*Business and Finance*, 6 February 1992).

The RTE strike was less of a crisis than the other disputes considered here; its aftermath was also less dramatic in terms of its impact on relative bargaining strengths of either side. But the dispute exhibited some of the characteristics common to the other semi-states under review. It also remains to be seen if the dispute "cleared the air" in terms of improving internal relationships.

A review of employee relations, chaired by Seán Healy, Director of Advisory Services at the Labour Relations Commission, is expected to advocate a number of changes in the way industrial relations are handled when it reports. As has already been established under the Special Adjudication Committee, which was set up by the Labour Court and which will cease after the review body has reported, some element of binding arbitration for major rows is expected to be recommended. In addition, a new worker participation initiative has also been launched within the station involving sub-board structures.

Irish Rail

Irish Rail faced its first national strike in almost 40 years in April 1994 in a row over work practice changes, the use of new ticketing equipment, new Japanese-built rail cars and 171 redundancies.

Management warned that non-acceptance of the changes meant that "maybe the railways could close for an indefinite period" and that Government investment of £270 million of European funding would be put in jeopardy. The dispute centred on compensation for cost-saving changes. Agreeing a formula was complicated by the locomotive drivers' pay system under which they were formerly paid one hour's basic pay for every 15 miles travelled over 140 miles. While locomotive drivers' average earnings in 1993 came to over £22,000, their basic pay stood at just over £11,200. The high overtime expectations of staff made it difficult to get a settlement formula. The first package to emerge from four weeks of Labour Relations Commission talks was overwhelmingly rejected and the row eventually went to the Labour Court.

Significantly, in a comprehensive audit on industrial relations in the semi-state two years earlier in February 1992, the Labour Relations Commission identified a number of features that were to emerge in the dispute. It found the company's management policy needed to be reviewed and that "while there are first class people available the present system did not appear to bring them to the forefront" (*Business and Finance*, 13 February 1992).

Both these issues surfaced strongly in the 1994 dispute in which 39 people were suspended for refusing to work the new arrangements before they had been agreed with the two major unions in the company, SIPTU and the National Bus and Rail Workers' Union (NBRU). The LRC report also suggested that the key personnel function at regional level needed to be examined and that there was a need for a specialist role separate from the operational aspects of the job. It also noted that relations between the various unions in the company must change or viability "will be put at risk" and that there were "too many shop stewards attending meetings".

Many of the key weaknesses identified in the LRC report emerged in the 1994 dispute. The introduction of imposed change on the ground was led by operational rather than personnel management, sometimes in a clumsy and high-handed fashion. Centrally, operational management around the chief executive were less than comfortable with being accused of breaching agreements and imposing change. During the conduct of the dispute their agenda appeared as if it were being set elsewhere — possibly in the Department of Transport, Energy and Communications in the wake of the Aer Lingus rescue.

The inter-union factor on the ground made the respective union leaderships reluctant to be seen to be the first to do business. Ironically, the National Bus and Rail Workers' Union, traditionally the more militant of the two unions in the company, appeared to be more strategically focused in terms of what they wanted from the outcome and in their acceptance of the ultimate need for change. Some problems arose with the handling of the SIPTU body, the National Rail Council, which recommended rejection of the final Labour Court terms, to the obvious unease of the full-time officials. Members at a grassroots level were urged by officials at key meetings to accept the terms. The final twist in the saga emerged with SIPTU workers overruling their own Rail Council and accepting the Labour Court recommendation while the National Bus and Rail Workers Union members, who had received no direction, rejected them. After the company warned that it had lost £1 million in freight business as a result of the strike threat (*Industrial Relations News* 17, 1994) and that 1,200 jobs could be lost if the strike went ahead, an agreement was eventually brokered with the help of ICTU assistant general secretary Kevin Duffy. The agreement preserved the bottom line of savings for the company.

Aer Lingus

In June 1992, the Chief Executive of Aer Lingus, Cathal Mullan, was predicting a return to profit despite continuing losses of over £40 million in the core air transport business. "It won't represent our career best, but we will make a substantial turnaround in this financial year" Mullan was quoted as saying (*Business and Finance*, 18 June 1992) after five years' losses in a row in the crucial air transport division. Four months later in October, then Transport Minister Máire Geoghegan-Quinn was to tell board members in no uncertain terms what she thought of the company's performance. With losses mounting, she openly declared after a board meeting that changes were going to have to start "at the top". Aer Lingus originally earmarked late October or November 1992 for the publication of its new rescue plan but it was to be delayed.

Two years earlier, at the height of the Gulf War, a smaller scale plan for recovery had been produced. The 1990 plan, the last element of which was only finally implemented in early 1992, sought to halve losses in air transport to £10 million through a combination of a pay freeze and cost cutting measures, offering a total saving of £20 million. After much haggling and several visits to the Labour Relations Commission and the Labour Court, this plan was finally accepted. But it proved to be too little too late and, significantly, when the next plan for the company emerged a definite deadline for the completion of talks was set providing finality. By late 1992 it was clear that the company was not going to meet its own deadline for the publication of its new Corporate Recovery Plan. Media speculation continued apace. The 1992 election and the change of Ministers was cited as the reason for the delay, but it became clear that what was being proposed was not being viewed as adequate by senior Government officials. It was no secret that relations between Aer Lingus and the Government had not been good in recent years. In fact it later emerged that the airline's first plan was rejected by the Government for not going far enough.

By the time the rescue plan was published in February 1993, its general details were well known and airline staff were accusing management of preparing them for the worst through "selective leaks". The plan pointed to the third successive year of losses of £40 million in the core air transport business but put these figures in the context of world-wide airline losses of $4 billion in 1991. The 16 page synopsis of the submission to Government blamed Ireland's peripherality on the edge of Europe, lack of a Dublin hub, seasonal business and the absence of a major home market for the airline's difficulties. Net losses for the year to March 1993 were forecast at £42 million, with restructuring charges of £18 million and losses on the company's investment in GPA bringing the figure to £91 million.

The synopsis outlined four options: the "bank driven" option with the loss of 4,000 jobs through the winding down of air transport; the "no Atlantic" option with the loss of 350 jobs; the core European operation with no Atlantic and finally the consolidation of services. The last recommended option involved cost savings of £24 million in 1993/94 through reducing payroll costs by £18 million and non-payroll costs by £6 million. The addition of a 10 per cent pay cut would have brought savings of a further £8 million. The option favoured at that point, for retaining 90 per cent of services, would have meant between 400 and 500 job cuts. The sale of four aircraft would have yielded £27 million and this overall strategy was based on the assumption that visitors carried into the country by the airline would have dropped by seven per cent.

Staff frustration at being kept in the dark about the first plan was directed at the Labour Party, largely for fairly vague commitments given by its leader Dick Spring at a meeting in the North

Terminal at Dublin Airport in the run up to the 1992 general election. These attacks later matured into a recognition that without the involvement of the Labour Party in Government there might be no equity injection at all.

The pace of events quickened in March 1993 with the departure of chief executive Cathal Mullan and of chief executive, passenger services, Kyrl Acton. Newly appointed executive chairman Bernie Cahill conceded that the company would not get the £400 million it had originally sought from the Government. The tough minded Cahill told union leaders that he wanted the airline to survive in its present form and that he had been given carte blanche by the Government to do what he felt was necessary. The Transport, Energy and Communications Minister, Brian Cowen, told the Dáil on the appointment of Cahill that the executive chairman must "take whatever action is necessary with immediate effect to restore the company to commercial viability". It was effectively a case of going back to the drawing board with the recovery plan. And he bluntly added: "We have sufficient analysis — now is the time for action". But the agony was not complete — in fact it was really only beginning. The Minister later put down clear markers for the restructuring operation, principally the maintenance of the Shannon stopover, which was later abandoned by Cahill to considerable political outcry and the defection of two TDs from the Fianna Fáil Parliamentary Party. But the Government's thinking was clear. The aim should be to make the core airline business viable, not to rely on subsidiaries to prop it up in counter-cyclical fashion. This represented a clear reversal of the policy pursued for the previous 30 years not alone at management level but at Ministerial level as well. When the "final" Recovery Plan, drawn up with the heavy involvement of former British Airways executive Peter Owen, ultimately emerged in July 1993, it caused consternation and sent shock waves among the workforce.

A week-end walk-out of about 1,000 ground staff — only 24 hours after details were announced — raised tensions but gave public expression to the private feelings of many workers. The plan warned in stark terms that if action was not taken to stem the huge £116 million losses projected, which included £44 million from the GPA write off, then "the Group will very quickly become insolvent" (Aer Lingus, *Strategy for the Future*, June 1993: 4). Losses were running at a rate of £1 million a week and banking facilities were being reduced as a result.

In addition to 1,500 job cuts — 1,280 in the airline — overtime was to be severely reduced, allowances were to be cut by over 50 per cent and a two year pay freeze was to be introduced. The plan proposed a total cost reduction of £50 million — £32 million of which was from payroll. The Government committed itself to an injection of £175 million but many observers believed that this was not enough in terms of the £539 million debt and the need to reduce gearing. The plan proposed three divisions within air transport: Aer Lingus, which would handle UK and European flights; Aer Lingus Shannon, which would operate transatlantic services, and Aer Lingus Express, a low cost low fare entrant on the Dublin-London market. Once the plan was published, and the Government commitment on £175 million equity made, it was clear that Ministers believed it was up to the management and the unions to reach agreement.

The message was that the future of the airline rested on the outcome of the bargaining process on the Cahill plan, with the Government having made their contribution. Initial trade union anger at the level of change being sought was later tempered by demands for equity participation and no compulsory redundancies. Weeks passed and further anger was vented before a three stage structure for talks was eventually agreed with SIPTU and separate arrangements were made with the Irish Airline Pilots Association. The departure of group personnel director, Jim Melly, sent out shock waves. But it also signalled a harder approach, particularly in the longer term. The later arrival of management consultant John Behan, formerly a consultant at Waterford Glass, only confirmed this view.

As well as proposing labour cost reductions of £34 million, the plan included the virtual elimination of overtime; a reduced rate of overtime pay of time and a quarter; reduced shift payments and roster duty allowances; the ability to use temporary and part-time staff and the concession of major flexibilities in working practices as well as flatter management and supervisory structures (see Table 1.1). Outsourcing and contracting out were also proposed for the catering area and some other support sections. A pay freeze until the end of 1995 was proposed and there was no commitment to pay the five and a quarter per cent still due from the PESP. Redeployment of staff was to be catered for through the creation of a new assessment centre. Overall, the company said that the level of the savings was not negotiable but it indicated that it was open to suggestions on how it could be achieved.

TABLE 1.1:
PAYROLL AND MANPOWER SAVINGS ACROSS
MAIN AREAS OF THE AIRLINE

Flight Services (including Cabin Crew)	£4.5 million	278 man-years *
Dublin Station	£5.4 million	314 man-years
Cork Station	£0.6 million	22 man-years
Shannon Station	£0.62 million	13.5 man-years
North America	$4.6 million	63 man-years (111 full-time jobs)
UK	£1 million	no change in jobs
Flight Operations (including pilots)	£3.1 million	125 man-years
Operational Control	£0.3m	12 man-years
Catering	£1.25 million (in-flight) & £0.5 million (staff restaurant)	164 man-years
Marketing Europe	£1.2 million	72 man-years
Cargo	£1.4 million	42 man-years
Information Technology	£0.7 million	26 man-years
Personnel (e.g. merging of functions also includes cleaning, transport and the medical centre)	£1.4 million	160 job losses approx.
Airline Finance	£0.4 million	29 man-years
Group Function	£1 million	35 man-years

* A "man-year" equates closely to a full-time job but not exactly. In the above table the total number of man years is 1,195 while the total number of proposed redundancies is 1,280 — excluding the 250 originally planned in TEAM. Source: *Industrial Relations News*, 28, 1993.

SIPTU, the largest union in the company, and the Irish Airline Pilots Association (IALPA) sought mandates to ballot for industrial action from their members in the wake of the publication of the Cahill Plan, largely as an insurance policy against imposed

change. In August 1993, the Labour Relations Commission, following consultations with all sides, put forward a talks formula based
on "best industrial relations practice". A separate Special Adjudication Board was to handle all issues which remained unresolved
by 31 October 1993, unlike 1990 when the normal industrial relations process proved to slow and cumbersome to deal with the aftermath of the Gulf crisis. Severance terms of four weeks pay for
the first ten years of service and six for the remainder were offered
with a limit of two and a half years salary. Improved early retire-
ment terms were later offered for people between the age of 50 and
55.

As it turned out, with the help of senior Labour Relations
Commission officials acting as conciliators, agreement in principle
for the vast bulk of the £21 million savings proposed by the company was reached by the end of the October deadline agreed for
the completion of negotiations. The level of concessions offered by
SIPTU in section by section negotiations on savings ultimately
allowed the company to take the pay cuts, including shift and duty
allowances, off the agenda. The level of change agreed was such
that rostered duty allowances, shift allowances, overtime pay
rates and bank holiday pay remained unchanged. SIPTU was also
able to claim victory in taking privatisation off the agenda. Concern was expressed by staff at the lack of apparent "pain" and
change imposed on management. This was to be a recurring theme
in the airline, not alone through its own crisis but through the
more prolonged difficulties in TEAM. The management strategy
was to get agreement from one key group, the pilots first, and then
put pressure on SIPTU to finalise negotiations. The final elements
of the Aer Lingus survival plan were later voted through by key
sections of the airline workforce but accepted subject to agreement
on a worker shareholding.

TEAM

Securing change and agreement on cost saving measures at the
Aer Lingus aircraft maintenance subsidiary TEAM proved the
most difficult piece of the overall group survival plan to put in
place. The battle between TEAM craft workers, management and
Government lasted for almost a year, monopolising the headlines
in newspapers and on TV, and exposed a facet of an industrial relations culture which many observers believed had disappeared 15
years earlier. The intractable dispute stood out for another reason
as an example of shop floor union power dominating and displac-

ing full-time union officials, reflecting a type of craftworker elitism that had largely been drowned out in an era of general unions and private sector rationalisations. But given the conditions under which TEAM was set up, particularly political intervention, and its inability to respond quickly to market changes, the dispute was probably inevitable. The underlying reasons for this protracted row, the severe weaknesses it exposed among management and unions and its implications, will be considered more fully in the next chapter. What concerns us here is a brief description of developments in what many considered to be a modern day Irish "miners' strike".

In late August 1993, TEAM Aer Lingus management tabled a £14 million cost cutting plan and warned that the company faced bankruptcy unless major change was agreed. The company, which employed almost 2,000 people, set out its difficulties in stark fashion and opened with the message "our business is in deep crisis". Staff were told that what they were being faced with was "no short term emergency caused by the absence of work and empty hangars". The market had changed, they were told, and the gap between TEAM's cost structure and the prices they sold work at meant they are "literally subsidising the maintenance of other airlines". This was later expressed in terms of getting down the cost per hour from £45 to £35. The message was that this situation provided a recipe for disaster. The Aer Lingus subsidiary had been severely hit by the downturn in the aviation industry. New investment combined with reductions in work required by the parent airline with the arrival of a new fleet "means that TEAM's committed customer base was now only 35 per cent of its current business capacity and only some 20 per cent of overall capacity".

Workers were told that when TEAM was established its prospects were bright, but that this was before the international recession. Competition had increased at a time when the market was contracting and larger airlines could sell excess maintenance capacity. Global alliances in the business had also lessened the opportunities for companies such as TEAM. New competition had only added to pressure on costs.

The document pointed out that new facilities such as Shannon Aerospace, British Airways in Cardiff and Lufthansa in Hamburg all had an expansion policy for third party work. Summarising the IR areas in which it needed movement, the company sought changes in work patterns, job booking, time clocking procedures and it also gave notice of a plan to terminate the productivity agreement by April 1994. The new arrangements were to be founded upon "truth in booking" designed to identify for management resolution shortfalls in support systems disrupting planned effective production and time which should properly be booked to overhead. The reduction in cost savings were to be achieved through cuts in overtime, which accounted for almost 30 per cent of total payroll, as well as roster duty allowances and a pay freeze on the final three and three quarter per cent due under the final phase of the PESP.

In fact, publication of the plan was just the beginning of a very rocky road to change in TEAM. In the summer of 1993, at a time when there was little work on hand, management had sought and received £1 million of Exchequer funding to take 300 staff who were laid off, back on the payroll for training. It was seen at the time as a cave-in by management under union pressure: in fact, earlier in 1993 in the wake of the currency crisis the company sought a temporary 15 per cent pay cut to help cushion them from a short interest rate rise on their then £47 million borrowings of up to 35 per cent. This was firmly resisted. Unions at TEAM were in somewhat of a unique position having no less than three "letters of comfort" guaranteeing their tenure and security of employment as Aer Lingus employees which they felt meant they could not be laid off. This was the price they had secured for 1,500 former craftsmen in the airline's mechanical and engineering section moving to TEAM when it was first established in April 1991. One was from the Minister for Transport of the day, Seamus Brennan. To the embarrassment of the ICTU leadership nationally, who saw TEAM as an example of a high tech and high pay job creation project, the craft unions rejected in three ballots the proposal to move to a gleaming new hangar. They later accepted it with some external union pressure.

TEAM was created out of a heady optimism generated by unprecedented growth in the airline business in the 1980s. The prediction was that numbers travelling would increase twice as fast as GDP — implying that numbers travelling by air would rise by five to six per cent per annum until the turn of the century. But this optimism proved unfounded and Western economies entered recession, presenting major difficulties for the fledgling company. As was noted later (Davy Stockbrokers, 1994: 3) "with the benefit of hindsight the timing could hardly have been less favourable". This report drawn up for Aer Lingus management noted:

In retrospect therefore, TEAM was launched at a time when many of the major world economies had already turned down and many others were on the brink of recession. In the event therefore, TEAM had, very early on to contend with market conditions, which were far less favourable than had been anticipated at the time of its formation.

Privately managers now concede that TEAM was largely created in response to political pressure from the Charles Haughey-led Government in the late 1980s for a high profile jobs project for North Dublin. The major mistake, as one senior executive flippantly noted later, was that they had not started it in Mayo or deepest Meath, far away from the largely inflexible culture of the mechanical and engineering section of the airline. Landing and take off facilities should not have been the sole consideration in deciding the location of the new operation, he maintained. In other words, a real greenfield situation would have been preferable, but traditional dependence on the airline as a major customer would have made this an unlikely option.

On the eve of the deadline for completion of the TEAM talks in February 1994, Director of Group Personnel John Behan warned employees that they could have a profitable business employing 1,700 people or become a "shadow of its former self" with job losses reaching 650. The major problem for the company was that it was seeking major change when its hangars were full of aircraft for the winter servicing schedule. Of the £14 million targeted savings, £3 million were to come from work practice changes as losses continued at £1 million a month.

After round the clock negotiations lasting over three days in the personnel building at Dublin Airport, the chairman of the craft workers groups of unions, Frank O'Reilly, alighted from the premises at close to 4.00 am, flanked by about 50 shop stewards, and declared a breakthrough. The company said it had achieved 95 per cent of the savings it sought but stressed that it reserved the right to audit what had been achieved and seek additional savings if necessary.

Discussions continued into early March and the unions held a ballot on work practice changes including a pay pause, although the management had been seeking a pay freeze. The issue of whether a formal agreement was reached in March 1994 was to loom large during the very public debacle over the company's future between TEAM unions, the Government and company management. Subsequent investigations by the Labour Relations

Commission and a Board of Assessors into the TEAM unions' plan believed that agreement had not been reached in March. Management later admitted that some elements of what had been negotiated with the unions, specifically night working, had in fact been implemented. Company executives suggested to the Joint Oireachtas Committee hearing on TEAM that the craft unions had in fact misrepresented the management position in the information packs handed out to shop floor workers in advance of a ballot.

Within three weeks of the original "agreement" between TEAM management and unions, company executives indicated they wanted additional savings after auditing what had been achieved in the first tranche of negotiations. In early April 1994 Aer Lingus executive chairman, Bernie Cahill, rejected the budget submitted by TEAM management, effectively signalling that the levels of changes which emerged from the talks process did not go far enough. John Behan indicated that the changes agreed so far "fall considerably short of producing the level of savings needed for TEAM to survive in its present form" (*Industrial Relations News* 14, 1994).

A new loop in the lengthy change process had begun, but in advance of tabling its new list of savings management launched a separate initiative to win supervisors over to the idea of change. While technically a management grade, the supervisors were highly unionised and had not really fulfilled a strictly management role. Contained in management's new cost saving proposals, launched in May 1994, was a demand for a 10 per cent pay cut. It also sought a new annualised hours shift system, under which staff would work 48 hours a week in winter and 40 in summer to match the peaks and valleys of the business cycle, as well as a pay freeze until 1995. The elimination of demarcation was also proposed as well as reductions in overtime from double time to time and a half and time and a half to become time and a quarter. Also, in May the appointment of Donnacha Hurley as the new chief executive of TEAM was announced. The company threatened 600 lay-offs but said that these could be avoided by acceptance of the second plan. The changes were aimed at bringing down the overall cost per man-hour from £44 to around £33. The unions had drawn up their own plan for the company which emphasised the need to grow the business and sought to reduce overall costs by increasing productivity and pushing up market share.

In advance of the European elections in early June, Enterprise and Employment Minister, Ruairi Quinn, asked the Labour Relations Commission to investigate the problems of TEAM Aer Lingus. His move was a reaction to the targeting of "the Northside Six" — the six Labour TDs who had been put under pressure from TEAM workers, including two who later did not vote with the Government on a crunch Dáil vote on the TEAM crisis. The Labour Relations Commission later issued a plan that largely backed management's proposals but dropped the idea of a 10 per cent pay cut and replaced it with a pay freeze until 1996. This report was rejected by the unions and subsequent efforts by the Commission to conciliate at the request of the Minister failed, although providing for an independent examination of the unions' plans. After the failure of the Labour Relations Commission initiative, and the revelation that TEAM would lose £10 million in the six months to September 1994, the ICTU intervened. After ten days of exploratory talks it got both sides to agree to an agenda which allowed for an independent Board of Assessors to be created to examine the unions' plans for TEAM and discussions on flexibility and other cost savings measures. Both sides agreed to attend the talks at the Marino Institute of Education in Dublin under the chairmanship of ICTU President Phil Flynn.

The agenda at the third formal effort to resolve the TEAM crisis adopted what was fundamentally a "carrot and stick approach". It offered the unions an agreed Board of Qualified Assessors to "analyse, quantify and report" on their plans. But any recommendation flowing from the Board could only be implemented after agreement had been reached on leave, working hours, how a pay freeze would operate, how flexible working arrangements would be introduced and on how temporary and contract work would contribute to meeting peak demands or specialist requirements. The talks broke up after two and a half weeks and after about 1,300 workers had been laid off progressively at TEAM. Management said that due to the lack of progress that had been achieved, it wanted to go to the Labour Court. Unions, on the other hand, argued they had made concessions that would have provided management with about 90 per cent of its required savings. In particular, they cited the concession of an offer of a 44-hour work week in winter. Management said that unions had failed to respond to bulk of the issues on its agenda. The most significant outcome of the ICTU process was that it narrowed the focus of the talks down to the management's agenda for cost savings.

The Board of Assessors' report fundamentally backed management's cost cutting approach, found a number of weaknesses in the union plan and highlighted the urgency of the situation facing the company. The Board said that the crafts unions' plans did "not provide an answer to the crisis in which TEAM finds itself" (*Report of the Board of Assessors*, 29 July 1994: 5.25). Unusually for a document which emerged from a union-initiated process, it backed the company's approach. It found that "the overall thrust of management's plan is to improve the cost base of the company to enable it to compete in the market and in particular to hold its share in an increasingly competitive environment". The Board believed that given the present state of TEAM and the market "this is the strategy capable of delivering survival".

The last lap of the dispute was to be a referral to the Labour Court which was allowed for in the ICTU agenda in the event of failure to reach agreement on the major issues. The Court basically backed the management on its demand for work practice changes but turned down demands for a 10 per cent reduction in basic rates of pay as well as changes in overtime and shift rates. The proposed pay freeze should run until 1996. It built on the Labour Relations Commission document hardening up in some areas and softened them in others. It backed the view of the earlier Board of Assessors' report that "there is evidence that management failed to manage and the workforce withdrew their consent to be managed". But it also recognised that its proposals "would delay the projected recovery period, nevertheless the court considers them essential to the resolution of the dispute" (LCR 14552: 7).

The unions went back to the Labour Court for clarification of the recommendation and subsequently recommended rejection, despite coded calls from ICTU President Phil Flynn for acceptance and warnings that it was the "end of the road". Mr Flynn and Denis Smyth, the crafts union spokesman, clashed publicly after Smyth alleged that the ICTU was part of an "unholy alliance" whose secret purpose was to privatise "vast swathes of the public sector" (*Irish Times*, 20 September 1994). Crafts union leaders later disassociated themselves from the remarks, but not before Flynn attacked the comments as "horseshit". The exchanges publicly highlighted the tension between the Congress and craft union leadership in the row.

Crafts union members rejected the Labour Court terms in their first vote by almost two to one, voting 308 to 528 against. SIPTU members had accepted them but the craftworkers' refusal to accept an aggregate vote meant that the overall acceptance could not stand. Within 48 hours of the rejection being declared, the company applied to the High Court to have accountant Hugh Cooney appointed as examiner on the basis of insolvency. In a dramatic development, days later, the unions decided to hold a new ballot which effectively reversed the earlier vote after some fairly general assurances were given by ICTU President Phil Flynn. Meetings later took place on an agreed return to work for the first 600 staff. In the end, it was a relatively transparent "fig-leaf" or pretext which allowed the unions to reverse their earlier decisive rejection. Some senior figures within Aer Lingus and TEAM wanted the interim examiner Hugh Cooney to "stay in" TEAM to review and reassess the Labour Court recommendation in the context of savings achieved and agreed — a bid for the component section and a proposal to bring the line maintenance area back into the airline.

Management had earlier committed themselves to accepting the Labour Court recommendation. Seeking to re-open the entire process could have had explosive consequences in the parent airline and given TEAM shop steward leaders, whose power base was in decline by the final stages of the dispute, a new lease of life. Aer Lingus' Director of Group Personnel, John Behan, is understood to have fought such a move fearing it would provoke major trouble on the ground and backwash into the airline in a way that could have sunk it. In his final report to the High Court before being withdrawn, the interim examiner Hugh Cooney urged that a three year peace agreement be introduced along with binding arbitration (*Business and Finance*, 13 October 1994). Management style would have to change "in a manner which will be evident to everyone". He also called for the rationalisation of trade unions structures within the company.

Having considered the development of what approximated a crisis in industrial relations in the bargaining systems of six semi-state companies, Chapter Two next looks at the roots of the current difficulties and the management and union responses to the emerging new agenda.

Chapter Two

ROOTS OF THE CURRENT CRISIS

Recent developments in the commercial semi-state companies under review throw up a myriad of issues relating to their role in a mixed economy: their corporate strategy in an era of increasing competition, the price they charge for their services to the wider economy and their social and strategic role in national development. What is of interest in the context of this book is the role of an industrial relations crisis in the development of overall personnel policy, how the crisis was managed and its longer term impact.

The roots of many of the crises under review arise from the impact of external changes coming up against entrenched and largely inflexible patterns of union organisation in the firms in question. The system of collective bargaining could simply not adapt in one move to the level of change being sought, much of it linked to rapidly changing market conditions or European deregulation. The tough and uncompromising approach of the State to commercialisation — as evidenced by the reluctance to inject large sums of taxpayers' funds into Aer Lingus, TEAM or Irish Steel, unless costs were reduced — meant that the Government had a large role in developments. Its reluctance to countenance continuing losses can be regarded as a trigger to the development of a number of the crisis disputes. Despite firm "targeting", particularly by the crafts unions in TEAM Aer Lingus and to a lesser extent by those in Irish Steel, the Government eventually held firm against a huge public outcry. The overall view appears to have been that the crisis in both firms represented "test cases" of the new Government approach and that backing down would produce problems down the line in other firms facing similar difficulties.

Most immediate attention has focused on the levels of job reductions that are planned in both ESB and Telecom Éireann in their quest to become more efficient and fitter organisations and to strengthen their ability to withstand direct competition. The notion of a semi-state job as solid secure employment may disappear forever. All of these questions relating to the role and management of commercial semi-state companies are likely to receive greater attention in future from both students and financial commentators mapping their general development. Of immediate interest here, as a prelude to examining developments in the ESB in greater detail, is to consider the pattern of the crisis in each company under a number of headings. Given the trauma attaching to each dispute for the management, the workforce and in some cases the public, the focus must be on the particular conditions, influences and rigidities within each group that spawned the crisis in the first place. The external driving forces of commercialisation and the changing face of political control of semi-states are also relevant as forces which shaped the agenda at the centre of the dispute. The common features that emerge in all the disputes will be discussed in the concluding section of the chapter.

Commercialisation

The need for greater commercialisation, arising out of both domestic and European pressure, emerges as one of main drivers of the painful change currently working its way through the commercial semi-state sector. But it was the lack of commercial activity in certain sectors of the economy which was to provide the stimulus, in the early years of the State, for the creation of State enterprise. Seán Lemass, one of the main architects of Ireland's two phases of industrial development in the 1930s and 1960s, believed that:

> State financed industries have been set up only where considerations of national policy were involved or where the projects were beyond the scope or unlikely to be undertaken by private enterprise (Sweeney, 1990: 3).

Lemass, very much a towering figure in terms of Irish industrial development, adopted this approach first as Minister for Industry and Commerce and later as Taoiseach. In effect, public enterprise was used as an arm of Government policy to make up for the lack of entrepreneurial drive among the existing business and property-owning classes. It was also used to fill a gap in the provision of vital goods and services which was not being catered for by the private sector. Thus the approach of the Government, particularly in the 1930s as part of the early phase of national reconstruction, was pragmatic rather than stemming from any specific ideological predisposition.

Fifty years later, following the collapse of Irish Shipping and doubts about the general role of State enterprise, the public attitude to semi-state companies had changed considerably. Lee (1989: 536), commenting on a Labour Party plan to create a National Development Corporation to supply a new dynamism to job creation, noted:

> With rapidly rising unemployment in the early 1980s it might seem as if this ambitious proposal for job creation would arouse enthusiasm. But the public had so lost confidence in the capacity of any State organisation to service any purpose except its own self-interest that the proposal generated more scepticism than enthusiasm.

Lee believed that poor returns on several enterprises and what he saw as an "apparent casualness" with which public sector trade unions resorted to the tactic of inflicting suffering on the public left public opinion increasingly dubious about the results of direct state intervention.

The National Planning Board (1984) identified five factors as contributing to the poor performance of semi-state companies: lack of clarity about their financial targets; the virtual absence of penalties for failure; the absence of any participation by actual decision makers in the risks attendant on their choices; the undertaking in particular of cases of investments on a scale disproportionate to the size of the company and the inevitable inability where companies were over-exposed because of such investments to weather the general economic recession.

Sweeney (1991: 17) found that there was a 24 per cent drop in numbers employed in 24 public enterprises between 1980 and 1990. In all, 21,288 jobs disappeared. The commercial semi-state sector, he says, "appears in the past to have been engaged in labour hoarding, that is, retaining workers on the payroll who were surplus to requirements of efficient operations". The pressure for greater commercialisation was two fold: an improvement in enterprise management and Government pressure for better performance because the national debt had exceeded £20 billion. Latest figures for semi-state employment confirm this downward employment trend. (See appendix I.)

Nevertheless, development of the State sector continued to be a significant plank of Government industrialisation policy right into the mid-1990s. The most recent national programme encompassing pay — the Programme for Competitiveness and Work —

agreed in early 1994, stressed that the most significant contribution which State enterprises could make to national economic and
social development was the delivery of services which are
"efficient, effective and able to compete in the markets they serve"
(Programme for Competitiveness and Work, 1994: 16).

The previous programme — the Programme for Economic and
Social Progress — noted that commercial semi-state companies
operated in every section of the economy and accounted for some
ten per cent of GDP and held assets of £9 billion. The PESP outlined eight principles for reducing constraints on the development
of commercial state companies and did not rule out private investment in State firms. Private involvement could consist of joint
ventures between State companies and private firms where suit-
able opportunities arose and where funding of the State company's
participation did not create difficulties for the company or the Exchequer.

Of the 24 commercial semi-state companies listed by Sweeney
(1991) six have either passed into private hands through privatisation, been subsumed by other semi-state companies or disappeared altogether through closure.

Even after the sale of Irish Life, B&I Line and Irish Sugar to
the private sector, the closure of Ceimicí Teo and Fóir Teo and the
demise of Irish Shipping, commercial semi-state companies still
account for a huge range of economic activity. Their activities encompass air and land transport, postal and telecommunications,
timber, electricity and gas as well as banking and broadcasting.
Some of the semi-states — notably the ESB and Telecom Éireann
— were up to recently considered to be natural monopolies because of the relatively small scale and size of the Irish market in
world terms. But changing technological advances, the advent of
the Single Market and the application of European Union competition rules to major utilities has changed the commercial logic
which made such firms a largely protected species.

The *Report of the Industrial Policy Review Group*, otherwise
known as the Culliton Report, claimed that "provided that the
commercial State enterprises are allowed to operate in a commercial manner, their contribution to the economy could become as
significant as it once was" (*Report of the Industrial Policy Review
Group* 1992: 75). But such a role could only re-emerge if they could
continue to make efficiency improvements which, Culliton noted,
some had achieved over the last decade. Overall, the report called
for innovative approaches to new products and markets, without

undue bureaucratic constraints or political intervention and provided they had access to the capital necessary for their expansion
on what he called a fully remunerating basis. But the report im-
plicitly recognised the clash between commercial and social objectives inherent in the running of many State firms. Their social role
had been financed through cross subsidisation from other parts of
the market served by such companies. Culliton, recognising the
contradiction of the commercial and social, noted:

> As a result these companies, including CIE and An Post and
> others have been placed in an increasingly difficult position,
> with the Government calling for increased profitability while
> insisting on the maintenance of what is often an ill-defined so-
> cial objective (*Report of the Industrial Policy Review Group*
> 1992: 75).

Both the Moriarty Task Force on Culliton and the overall Government response was much more circumscribed than the original
report itself. So much so that Denis Hanrahan, a member of the
Moriarty Task Force, while agreeing with a recommendation to
appoint better qualified people to semi-state boards felt that the
approach on the relationship with Government was too restrictive.

Arising from this report the Government accepted that State
enterprises and their sponsoring departments should agree clear
commercial mission statements published in their annual reports.
Benchmarking of the prices and charges of State enterprises as
part of a process to meet absolute standards for competitiveness of
their prices and services was also to be introduced. As we have
already seen, An Post's plan to close 550 sub post offices as part of
its original Viability Plan was shot down by the Minister of the
day, Seamus Brennan, because of its impact on rural communities.
The initial Cahill Plan for Aer Lingus involved the maintenance of
the controversial Shannon stopover. The company had been asked
to draw up its original blueprint while leaving the stopover in
place. It was later partly altered, but the airline subsequently
modified its policy again with hints of a political accommodation.

The other major force for commercialisation has been European
Union-sponsored deregulation and the application of the rules of
the Treaty of Rome through competition policy. This has figured
largely in the plans of the ESB to reduce costs under the threat of
the arrival of independent power producers (IPPs) or the less immediate threat of third party access by foreign utilities to the Irish
electricity grid. The new Government policy of benchmarking of

prices and charges and the internal benchmarking of working
practices and output per worker in such companies as Telecom and
the ESB only adds to this pressure. Additional external pressures
have arisen in the cases of Irish Rail, Irish Steel and Aer Lingus
as a result of their application for some EU funding to get them
over their difficulties. Rationalisation measures are being demanded in advance of any exceptional EU funding to these firms,
applying a new external pressure on the industrial relations
agenda.

For now the jury is very much out on how commercial the Government actually wants semi-state companies to be. Even with the
injection of £25 million or more, Irish Steel is unlikely to be viable
in the short to medium term but the same cannot be said of the
other firms seeking support. While the TEAM Aer Lingus crisis
was fundamentally about viability, and, as we shall see later,
whether it was "manageable", the Irish Steel rescue aimed more at
bare survival. Even the Labour Court recognised that the company would not be viable in the strict commercial sense in the
longer term. Thus semi-state management — much of it more
used to operating within the strictly nationally set parameters —
is working to a new set of commercial pressures, the implications
of which they are only now assessing and coming to terms with.

The Irish Congress of Trades Unions recognised many of the
changing realities facing semi-states with in its major policy
statement "Public Enterprise and the Economy" issued in 1990. In
summary, the new policy recognised that the traditional position
of outright opposition to all forms of privatisation was no longer
adequate. While opposing the selling-off of Government shares in
public enterprises, it supported the establishment of joint ventures between State companies and firms in the private sector;
channelling private investment into public enterprises through
investment companies along the lines of Irish Telecommunications
Investment and maintaining public control of strategic public enterprises. It sought the extension of the activities of public enterprise into new areas of job creation and the selection of publicly
owned firms to develop large scale indigenous companies capable
of exploiting the European market. The ICTU accepted the need to
sell off a minority of Government shares in public enterprise
where there was no alternative method of raising the capital to
make existing jobs more secure or create new ones.

The Union Response

Traditional semi-state union organisation, much of it based within crafts unions, has had great difficulty coming to terms with the new industrial relations agenda produced by the sharper commercial pressures on State companies. Heavily committed to the adversarial way of doing business, much of the power and strong organisation of such unions has been predicated in the past on their position within monopoly companies. But their role in semi-state companies is in a state of flux as demonstrated by the early reaction of ESB unions to the McKinsey job shedding proposals and the eventual acceptance of change within Aer Lingus itself. And while it is too early to predict the future shape of management/union relations in such companies, different approaches are likely to emerge in which general unions may take the lead. Recent calls for new definitions of leadership and of the need for "quality leadership", from the ICTU President Phil Flynn, suggest a questioning of the traditionally accepted principle of "leading from behind". His statement, (*Irish Independent*, 5 October 1994) following the crises in Irish Steel and TEAM Aer Lingus, implies a serious unease over some traditional union approaches to the new wave of restructuring and rationalisation demands. The creation of an ICTU review group to examine the unions' handling of change in such instances may create an expectation that new thinking can be implanted in every local dispute about change. But as several leading figures admitted privately, after the TEAM and Irish Steel disputes, strong unions need strong managers which suggests a symbiotic relationship.

The landscape of change within semi-states has, however, not been entirely unremittingly negative: major rationalisation programmes, some of them utilising innovative working patterns, have emerged in such companies as Bord Gáis, Bord na Móna and ACC Bank. In many cases job shedding and flexible working arrangements were introduced without a single dispute and negotiated with the unions signing up for agreements that included contracting out of services. The structure, business and location of many of these companies meant their difficulties did not receive the same levels of public attention as those of the semi-states which hit the headlines in 1994. The factors that make severe change acceptable in one state organisation and not others is worthy of a separate comparative study. But the degree of planning involved, company culture, the nature and location of the business as well as the history of management/union relations are likely to emerge as major influences.

The emergence of pay cuts on the agenda for rationalisation has caused the greatest problems, particularly at TEAM and Irish Steel. Aer Lingus stands out as an example of where the unions adopted a more strategic approach, linking concessions on work practice changes to the wider equity issue and managing to negotiate pay cuts off the table. The unprecedented level of change demanded within the companies under review has put severe strains on the more conventional type of trade union leadership that has operated within these firms.

Much of this style of leadership has emphasised the role of unions as guardians and protectors of agreements which were framed under different economic conditions to those operating today. The concentration was very much on internal developments within the company itself in terms of protecting the position vis à vis other groups and operating within a highly proceduralised system of rules and processes which were almost exclusively inward looking. The very technical nature of the businesses involved — television production, steel manufacture or the generation of electricity — was seen to justify and sanction this approach and, as in the case of the ESB, to warrant special arbitration machinery from Government.

The creation of Groups of Unions within these enterprises, which were exclusively devoted to aggregating and co-ordinating the unions' demands within the operation, further bolstered the internalisation of the system of industrial relations. The old disputes procedure within RTE, under which unions not in dispute would only accept direction from designated managers, is an anachronism from this era. In this climate the company itself is in effect the bargaining unit and what happens outside is of little direct consequence. The monopoly status of most of the firms in question tended to underscore this approach. The external competitive pressures that were needed to keep the system in check and provide an equilibrium to the monopoly power of the unions in some of these concerns were absent until recently.

Significantly, those businesses that faced the greatest direct competition, such as Aer Lingus, were able to achieve change with the least disruption. Day to day experience of cut throat competition on the ground may have conditioned staff to accept greater change but a more sophisticated level of union leadership, aware of commercial and economic realities, also played a part. Developments within Aer Lingus and TEAM provide starkly contrasting approaches to the handling of change by union leaderships. One figure close to both rows said that there were visible signs of change in Aer Lingus and people had been conditioned to the fact that more was coming. In TEAM, the very opposite was the case: staff were constantly being told "how great they were" and weak management had helped the shop stewards become the dominant force. Planning and conditioning were cited as the key ingredient to any successful change programme, with Guinness being a prime example in the private sector.

The crafts union approach within TEAM demonstrated an almost theological obsession with procedure and maintaining agreements, as well as an example of shop steward dominance over full-time officials. The agenda in Aer Lingus was much more influenced by the full-time officials and fundamentally more strategic; no compulsory redundancies or pay cuts but discussions on everything else. TDs were targeted to win support for an equity stake and SIPTU switched the emphasis to negotiated change. As senior SIPTU official Paul O'Sullivan told the *Industrial Relations News* Conference in March 1994:

> We put forward the idea that agreement required three parties, the Government for equity, the management for a plan as well as a staff contribution. We were aware of new management and the personalities that were coming who prefaced a major shift in the way IR was done in the airline (*Industrial Relations News*, 1994, Conference Report: 14).

Within Aer Lingus, SIPTU almost took ownership of the Cahill Plan by linking their acceptance with an inherent belief in the future of the company itself and their role in it. Despite having agreed a two stage negotiation process, with unresolved issues going to a special tribunal, the bulk of the changes were agreed directly with management across the table with the help of the Labour Relations Commission.

To what extent has the so-called "crafts union mentality" of resistance to change surfaced in these disputes? During the TEAM dispute some crafts union leaders made clear that they saw the row within the aircraft maintenance company as having wider implications: it was an effort to undermine "the notion and principle of the craft" in all the semi-states. They painted the TEAM row, and the level of change being sought, as effectively a trial run for the sort of unacceptable demands that were going to surface down the line in both the ESB and Telecom Éireann. Efforts to lay the ground for a national craftworker stoppage by using the Dub-

lin Council of Trades Unions as a platform were blocked by a
number of other unions on procedural grounds. In reality, few of
the other union leaderships, and in particular the ICTU, were
keen to back such a strategy which was led by some of the more
militant union figures.

The type of militancy which surfaced during the TEAM row
had definite rings of the past to it. Some of the central figures on
the union side clearly saw it as a last stand of the crafts unions in
the face of changes which were set to unravel their traditional
bargaining power and status. Overall, during the dispute, apart
from the general publicity generated by their own plan which was
largely found wanting by the ICTU's Board of Assessors, it was
hard to see the TEAM shop stewards as having any real strategy
or fallback position. They appeared to believe that targeting the
politicians would remove the need for the sort of change demanded
by the management and almost ignored the reality of the £1 million a month level of losses or the damage to the business from a
prolonged dispute.

At the root of the long deadlocked dispute was the overhang of
mismanagement which went back to when TEAM was founded,
but also back to the Mechanical and Engineering Section of Aer
Lingus itself, out of which TEAM was developed. In retrospect
TEAM may emerge as one of the last fighting stands of the crafts
unions whose influence has been on the wane for some years. The
former ICTU general secretary, Donal Nevin, recognised the decline in influence and strength of the crafts unions *vis-à-vis* their
general union counterparts. Nevin believed that their decline was
probably the most enduring legacy of the 1969 maintenance men's
dispute which put more than 30,000 people out of work throughout the country. While they had won the immediate pay battle of
that momentous dispute, they had lost the war because the employers never again bargained with the craftsmen as a cohesive
negotiating unit. He noted:

> Perhaps as important as the decline in craft power was the si-
> multaneous rise in the influence of semi-state employees who,
> in the 1960s became for the first time a critical factor in pay de-
> termination because of their size, their high level of trade union
> organisation and the industrial power they had derived from
> providing crucial public utility services (Chubb, 1992: 129).

Paul Sweeney, an economist with SIPTU, while recognising the
huge job losses within the semi-states during the 1980s when

about one job in four disappeared, says that both sides failed to "shape up" for changes. There was a cosy relationship between trade unions and employers in many semi-states based on a view that they would always be bailed out. He believes that some of this passivity arose from the monopoly status of the businesses involved. He noted:

> The unions in the semi-states have been cushioned and most of them have not realised there is a need for change. It is often up to the individual official. Our own colleagues often tell us to leave well enough alone when we call for change and push people to move.[1]

Sweeney believes there are two major drivers of change: technology and European Union deregulation. Some union officials in the private sector have taken more of a proactive role than their colleagues in the semi-state sector in terms of handling and shaping up to change. Many of the semi-states end up going for what he calls "cataclysmic rather than gradual" change. Moving earlier on the acceptance of some pain would probably result in the saving of jobs and an avoidance of a repeat of the job shedding of the 1980s. In the future good trade union leadership may have to think ahead, give some leadership and stress that if you "do the business with management before a crisis" through getting rid of overtime and consolidating into the rate in return for flexibility, they would be better off. Sweeney, who has broad experience and has made an input into some major rationalisations faced by members of his own union, says that some shop stewards can conceive of the notion of leading change and taking a more proactive stance, but others cannot. In Irish Steel, he said SIPTU had called for the original viability report from accountants Simpson Xavier Horwath Consulting which was commissioned by the Minister for Enterprise and Employment. In retrospect, this should have been done in 1985.

Another key question that has to be asked is why crafts unions in the private sector have managed to accommodate change without resource to disputes, while the very same unions in the public sector have led the battle lines for resistance. The answer probably has something to do with conditioning, a different management approach and the "job for life" mentality of some workers in the public sector. Resistance to change has not, however, been uni-

---

[1] In an interview with the author, 1994.

versal in the public sector and different responses have emerged in different firms. Significantly, crafts unions represented well less than ten per cent of the workforces in the 12 companies considered in the ICTU *New Forms of Work Organisation Report* issued in 1993. In TEAM Aer Lingus, however, they accounted for almost half those on the payroll, suggesting a possible link between crafts union density in particular firms and patterns of resistance.

One trade union official with responsibility for workers in the ESB believed that the new types of agenda being pushed by management put union figures in a new role. They "became the meat in the sandwich" between a management demanding new and unprecedented levels of change and a workforce who were resisting it. In the new environment they had to facilitate change rather than resist it but aim to maintain core conditions.

Another difficulty for the unions is that some of the officials looking after semi-state firms have themselves come from the industry they are now overseeing. While this gives them greater familiarity with day to day issues and personalities, it can often make it more difficult for them to stand back, bring fresh thinking to the job and carve out a leadership role. This "inbreeding" amongst the union leadership, which is also reflected on the management side, further contributes to the internalisation of rows in which outside, commercial or comparative analysis is lacking.

The multi-union factor has emerged in a number of disputes under consideration, particularly TEAM, Irish Rail and Irish Steel. In both TEAM and Irish Steel the crafts unions displayed an abhorrence of negotiating around the table with SIPTU. This friction between the craft and general union outlook was particularly pronounced at TEAM, where the SIPTU clerical workers were the first and only group to accept the terms of the Labour Relations Commission peace formula. This disdain for SIPTU was also reflected in the attitude of the shop steward-led leadership in TEAM for the ICTU itself, and particularly for the fairly muted Congress leadership call for an end to the disruption during the dispute and the inconveniencing of the public. The tension between SIPTU and the National Bus and Railworkers Union was less intense, but it probably delayed the settlement of the 1994 dispute. One side effect of both the TEAM and Irish Rail disputes could be to widen the gap between craft and general unions and with the ICTU itself, which at times appeared impotent in influencing developments in both rows.

One common feature of the disputes under review is the role of the Irish Congress of Trade Unions. The Congress become involved to a greater or lesser extent in most of the restructuring rows of recent years and had a particularly high profile in the summer of 1994 as a result of the Irish Steel and TEAM disputes. The reasoning behind such interventions is probably three-fold: to help and assist unions where they are having difficulty on the ground or where there is weak leadership locally; to avoid rows with an inter-union dimension and more generally to avoid the general trade union movement getting a "bad name" through high profile disputes which threaten public services.

The complexity of both the TEAM and Irish Steel disputes always suggested that they were unlikely to be resolved by just one intervention and that they would "go to the wire" and be subject to several different peace initiatives. Some senior figures tend to see the ICTU-initiated interventions in both disputes in terms of bringing the established statutory dispute solving agencies, like the Labour Court and Labour Relations Commission, into disrepute. This belief is based on the view that the expectation of another "loop" to the peace process will make the unions less likely to agree a final settlement, if the safety net of last ditch ICTU intervention is known to exist. The Congress, however, increasingly sees its role as charting a future for unions and giving leadership in times of crisis and major waves of change on the shop floor, which its satellites may have difficulty coming to terms with. The ICTU would also argue that as a social partner and signatory to the Programme for Competitiveness and Work it is obliged and expected to play a part in maintaining industrial peace. The risk, however, is that the public will always expect such interventions to succeed.

Management and the Changing Political Regulation

Apart from the momentous liquidation of Irish Shipping, few recent Government decisions have had as much impact as the rejection of the first rescue plan for Aer Lingus. The decision by the Minister for Transport, Energy and Communications, Brian Cowen, in February 1993 was a public rebuttal of the combined rescue blueprint developed by both the board and executive team at the airline. It signalled a tougher and more determined approach to the emerging crisis at the airline after some months dithering in late 1992 due to the general election.

The decision also cast the die for the handling of the emerging difficulties in the other semi-states, particularly Irish Rail and Irish Steel. The message was that the Government would sanction additional funding, but only after both sides came together with a plan that would make the operation viable. But whether it amounted to a new strategy for dealing with the semi-states or was just another version of crisis management is another issue. Threats to put Irish Steel into liquidation, and the appointment of an examiner to run TEAM after the rejection of the Labour Court terms, appeared to confirm the hardening of approach. Both developments also provoked shock among the unions, even if the reaction in the Irish Steel case was somewhat delayed. Recent comments by the Minister Cowen (Dáil Éireann Report, 4 March 1994) that the core function of the semi-states is in the delivery of services which are efficient, effective and able to compete in the markets they service indicates the Government's overall approach in the post-Culliton era. The approach to each individual company by its parent Department can vary considerably. According to Paul Sweeney, the Exchequer can often be a poor shareholder:

> In a private company, the shareholders want to stay in the business, grow the operation, make money and pay the wages. Politicians have an agenda which is unstable and will diverge from the ordinary agenda of management regularly and sometimes in a way that is hard to predict. There is a need for more independent members on semi-state boards.[2]

The issue here is to what extent pressure for deregulation, greater commercialisation and the advent of the crisis in major firms has altered the traditional tripartite relationship between the major actors in the semi-states, the Government, the management and the unions. A more "hands-off" approach by Government appears to be emerging, in which it will leave any direct intervention until the latest possible hour. But given the political sensitivities attaching to particular decisions and the huge role of semi-state companies in maintaining the social and economic fabric of rural Ireland, Government will never be a neutral party. The handling of the future of the Midlands peat stations in the ESB could be a test case. Rather than disappearing altogether, the nature of political control over semi-states may be on a different basis in future and be less of a knee jerk response and more subtle.

---

[2] In an interview with the author, 1994.

The Industrial Policy Review Group found a "more general and apparently pervasive problem" reported to it regarding the relationship between the Government and the semi-state enterprises. It reported "excessive involvement" of Government in operational matters concerning the enterprises. It also believed that:

> By giving the enterprise a clear mandate and adequately briefing appointees to the boards of directors in advance, the Government should have no need to make frequent interventions on matters of detail (*Report of the Industrial Policy Review Group*, 1992: 75)

Board appointments should be based solely on the criteria of the ability of the people concerned to contribute to the direction of the enterprise, it stressed. All of the above raises the question of the scope of management to manage and make mistakes in critical situations as well as about the level of central Government supervision. Was Government interference in the past based on a lack of trust of those in high places in State firms, or pure political expediency and a determination to avoid the political flak from hard decisions? New chief executive appointees, hired on salaries in excess of traditional pay norms, are likely to take less kindly to old style interventions, having been provided with a strictly commercial mandate.

One of the key issues to emerge from an examination of developments in semi-state companies in recent years concerns the ability of "home grown" management or of executives who have come up through the system to handle the more commercial challenges or even a crisis in the operations under their own control. Traditionally, many of the chief executives of semi-states came from "within the fold" rising through the ranks to take the top job having served an apprenticeship and having gained skills in other areas. The question here is whether chief executives from outside the culture are better equipped than those who have grown up within it to steer the operation through the choppy waters of deregulation and into a more commercially-driven environment. Irish Steel, TEAM, Aer Lingus and An Post have gone this route, while the crises in the ESB and RTE have left the existing management team largely intact.

One senior figure interviewed blamed much of the difficulty in Aer Lingus and TEAM and within semi-states generally on "introspective management" whose primary concern was their own position, on where the power lay within their own organisation and where the threats to it were coming from. He also blamed some of the situation within the public sector on the lack of penalty for non-performance for those at the top and the lack of reward for real achievement. External pressures and crises were often needed to force vital readjustment to changing conditions.

Government policy appears to be to gradually replace many of the current generation of chief executives who have emerged from within the firm by outsiders from the private sector. Back in 1985 Brian Patterson, then with the Irish Management Institute, said the fact that semi-state chief executives kept up their commitment and performance despite "anti-market policies" and rigid controls on pay surely made them the "corporate Saints of Ireland" (*Business and Finance*, 2 May 1985). By 1994, both the roles of semi-state chief executives and the public perception of them had changed considerably.

One close observer of the situation in TEAM prior to its difficulties said that so lacking was the firm in a management structure, particularly at front line level, that it was an organisation in "free-fall". While highly successful at marketing, the weaknesses in the structure of TEAM since its creation appeared to have escaped the highest echelons within the airline.

Divisionalisation, while improving the lot of some firms had not worked in others; the breaking up of CIE is generally regarded as a positive move, but Dublin Bus is probably better managed than either Irish Rail or Bus Éireann. And while McKinsey in the ESB suggested that the hiring of new executives be used to signal the level of change, this has not occurred as the bulk of appointees to the five new divisions in the company are internal. Restructuring within Aer Lingus has been accompanied by a whole range of internal appointments at mid-management level. This has damaged the credibility of senior management in the eyes of those at ground level who have taken the change and created a lack of transparency in the promotion system. Significantly, many, including those who would not have supported his style of management, believe that former British Airways executive Peter Owen, who was drafted in to implement the Cahill Plan in Aer Lingus, left too quickly. Installed as chief executive in early 1993, he spent only a year in the company. His knowledge of the business was seen as too valuable an asset to lose. Owen and Bernie Cahill, the straight talking Cork-born Executive Chairman, were rumoured not to have seen eye to eye on a number of issues as time went on.

Government willingness to "take the heat" on major job shedding and work practice changes in semi-state companies in turn modifies their relationships with unions. It effectively alters the political exchange that has operated between Government and unions and puts more emphasis on the management/union side of the bargain. The unions in TEAM Aer Lingus targeted the politicians right through the various interventions on their dispute, and at one stage managed to lose the Labour Party two votes in a crucial Dáil vote in the row. But as time went on, politicians, even those who had openly supported the demands of the TEAM workers, were growing noticeably less patient with their approach, particularly after the unions' own plan had been examined and been found wanting. Both management and the full-time union officials regarded the pressure on politicians as a "cul de sac" which avoided the real issues being faced. Business was only finally done when the political avenue was perceived to be futile.

Challenges to the Established Industrial Relations Process

Most of the crises under review emerged as a result of the standard collective bargaining process being unable to cope with the level of change demanded under the pressures of cost cutting and greater deregulation. The specific nature of the changes in work practices demanded varied in each case, but all represented a profound challenge and undermining of the standard work patterns and their replacement with more flexible arrangements, new manning or atypical forms of working. Some elements of what has been sought are associated with human resource management strategies for change and the creation of flexible workforces. But in a number of the cases under review, the changes were sought as part of the collective bargaining agenda rather than as elements of a fully blown human resource management initiative. The ESB, as shall be explained later, represents a case of a company which moved comprehensively into a human resource management initiative following the 1991 crisis.

In fact, TEAM provides a good public sector example of HRM gone wrong or of a management deluding themselves into thinking they had an open relationship with their workforce and of benefiting from the follow through in terms of flexibility. Just before the storm clouds gathered for TEAM back in late 1992, one senior figure said his company's approach to human resource management was "costly, frustrating, slow moving and intensive in terms of management, staff and communications". Despite various production problems on the ground and unscheduled work stoppages in early 1993, management continued to insist publicly that there was no militancy at the company. Not alone were TEAM executives' financial and profit projections for TEAM too optimistic, but their assessment of the determination of their own workforce to resist change was wide of the mark. A report by the consultants Stoy Hayward presented to the Oireachtas Committee in June 1994 said that in the course of their work the previous year "we formed the view that the company's senior management, although strong in the areas of marketing and engineering gave insufficient priority to other commercial issues and finance". High overtime payments also tended to destabilise working relations between unions and management within the firm by creating unreal expectations of earnings.

Conclusion

Forces contributing to the rapid level of change within semi-state companies considered in this chapter include commercialisation, de-regulation and the changing nature of Government and political control. The history of developments at Irish Steel, An Post, RTE, Irish Rail, Aer Lingus and TEAM point up a number of lines of challenge to existing workplace patterns and traditional methods of dispute resolution. Some of the challenges relate to numerical flexibility, as in the case of An Post, and the use of contract workers which represents a threat to the internal logic which has underpinned unions' total bargaining approach in many of the firms under consideration. These demands have threatened the unions' management and protection of regular work patterns within these establishments. A second line of challenge to emerge within Irish Steel and TEAM confronts the inflexibilities of crafts unions and their inability to accept tasks not related to their pure concept of their craft. In Irish Steel this arose with the demand for "cross-fertilisation" and in TEAM with the request to "work up" to all categories of supervisor and do so-called "housekeeping duties". Some of the challenges that have emerged come under the heading of what is often referred to as numerical flexibility or emphasis on the flexible use of employees. While developments in Irish Steel in relation to cross-fertilisation, in An Post in relation to part-time and temporary workers and in TEAM in relation to flexibility of functions represent separate strands of the challenge in each of these companies, the most developed and sustained challenge embracing all these strands together has emerged in the ESB.

This strongest and third line of challenge to the conventional industrial relations model has emerged within ESB in terms of demands for management de-layering, a major cut in numbers and radical alterations in work practices combined with the extensive use of outside contractors in both generation and distribution.

The McKinsey proposals for the ESB are being introduced in the Board against the backdrop of a major reassessment of the roles of management and unions triggered by the four day 1991 dispute, one of the most crippling strikes in the history of the State. This strike led to a serious questioning of existing bargaining relations and the later introduction of a "soft" human resource policy by management which emphasised participation, trust and joint goal setting, separated out from traditional industrial relations issues. Thus while some developments in the companies under review have posed threats to the standard bargaining agenda, difficulties were eventually resolved within the framework of conventional industrial relations. The ESB, on the other hand, presents us with the case of a company where, in the aftermath of the 1991 dispute, the key actors moved relations onto a new plane and to an integrated platform for the introduction of human resource management. The new agenda within ESB presents one of the strongest challenges to the dominance of the collective bargaining model to emerge in the semi-state sector so far, but in the context of a new model of relations.

Developments within the companies under review illustrate the problems of introducing separate and discrete strands of change; the new agenda being promoted within ESB presents us with a multi-stranded approach in the context of an elaborate and ambitious model for relations. The company is seeking to introduce elements of change found separately in all the companies considered here, but simultaneously. The conditions which produced the crisis in the Board's collective bargaining system and which ultimately led to the implanting of a new model of management/union relations are the subject of this book.

The level of trauma experienced in handling change in the companies considered here highlights the complexity of bedding-in new work practices and work patterns in firms with very structured but traditional forms of union organisation. The roots of the crisis were different in a number of the cases considered, reflecting different degrees of external and internal pressure. The disputes in both RTE and An Post were largely the product of market pressure arising from a new focus on cutting costs. The ESB case, however, highlights an internal crisis taking place against a background of mounting external de-regulatory pressure. The 1991 dispute not only triggered a serious review of internal relationships, leading to transformation, but was a catalyst for an external examination on structures and costs, with unprecedented consequences. After a brief outline of the work of the major writers on industrial relations theory in the next chapter, the roots of the 1991 strike in the ESB will be considered.

Chapter Three

THE DEVELOPMENT OF INDUSTRIAL RELATIONS THEORY

To understand the impact of the new range of forces bearing down on semi-state companies considered in the first two chapters, and on developments in the ESB in particular, an overview of the main strands of theoretical literature on management strategy and industrial relations is outlined here.

The disputes considered in Chapter One provide an example of a collective bargaining agenda that had severe difficulty coping with and adjusting to new demands being sought, in terms of changes to workplace rules and regulations. Formalised working arrangements, codified in long standing agreements, were in many cases being dispensed with and overwhelmed by forces outside of union/management control and in some cases outside domestic control. Traditional approaches to dispute resolution also proved to be too slow and cumbersome in dealing with the more market-driven agendas which require rapid adjustment to change.

Industrial relations systems and procedures in all the semi-state companies, especially the ESB, represent examples of a form of industrial relations known in the academic literature as pluralism. Within pluralism, the basis for good industrial relations is to be found in the jointly agreed rules and regulations which form the foundation for the conduct of employment relations. While this model has held a dominant place for the last three decades, in recent times it has come under attack from a number of directions, including those who advocate a shift to a system which de-emphasizes the role of collective bargaining.

Disputes in RTE, Irish Steel, An Post, Irish Rail, TEAM and Aer Lingus all represent bargaining agendas that have reached breaking point under the new more commercially-driven forces now ranged on semi-state companies. The new demands represent a challenge to the pluralist orthodoxy which has dominated management/union relations in these firms and up to now largely delivered the goods without major disruption.

But the weaknesses exposed by these disputes raise very serious questions about the ability of traditional collective bargaining to cope with the new pressures and its suitability in an era of market-driven change and deregulation. Elements of the new human resource management approach, including numerical flexibility and demands for new and atypical forms of working, have emerged in many of these firms.

The history of bargaining in the ESB in the 1980s, which will be outlined in the next chapter, and the break that was partly engineered by the 1991 dispute, encompass in microcosm the changes now underway elsewhere. While electricians' pay was the central issue in 1991, the dispute exposed an internal management agenda trying unsuccessfully to come to grips with European de-regulation, the erosion of surplus capacity and increasing concern over price. The 1980s was an era of significant industrial relations difficulty for the Board and witnessed the break down of bargaining relationships at a number of levels. But the shock to the system generated by the 1991 dispute was a catalyst for major change both internally and externally. It accelerated the break up of the Board into five units under threats from Government and produced a switch to a human resource management policy throughout the company which emphasised flexibility, trust and the need to adjust to the new changes.

The new change agenda outlined by McKinsey for ESB, based on the scrapping of existing agreements, shift premia and in many cases secure conditions, is a major test of the transformed industrial relations climate forged by the 1991 dispute. The framework for the new model of relations, based on the Cassells Committee report will be considered in Chapter Seven. In the context of the disputes considered in the first section of this book, and the future evolution of bargaining in semi-states generally, developments within ESB highlight in great detail efforts by the one of the country's largest and strategically most important employers to handle the new agenda.

The literature on the development of pluralist collective bargaining points to a series of environmental factors that influence the shaping of management strategy. However, one of the areas ignored is the role of a major strike as a catalyst for transformation or as a mechanism which changes the pluralist ground rules. The shattering strike animated in the most public way a number of weaknesses in the Board's bargaining structure, some of which had appeared in previous disputes. The significance of the 1991 strike is that it gave expression to several of these key areas of deadlock which had not been resolved before, at the one time, thereby accelerating the force for transformation and change. It exposed a crisis in the system of industrial relations the Board has operated since 1969, instituted after the Fogarty Committee report. Fogarty effectively mapped the future course for management/union relations in his seminal report completed in the wake of a series of turbulent disputes in the 1960s.

The ESB electricians' strike of April 1991 exposed in graphic detail the shortcomings in the system of industrial relations the Board had operated since 1969. It ultimately led to a major initiative to supplant and replace the existing system of personnel management with a model which is a combination of traditional collective bargaining and human resource management. The April 1991 dispute brought into open relief for the first time the serious misgivings that had been held by management about the system of industrial relations operated by the Board since the early 1980s, particularly in regard to its ability to deliver change and respond to new external conditions.

The development of personnel policy in the ESB, from its first expression as a Board staff section in 1935 to the formal setting up of a fully fledged Personnel department in the late 1960s, conformed to pluralistic principles. From the pay Tribunals of the early and late 1940s to the Joint Industrial Council which was set up in 1970, the Board's system of adversarial industrial relations was based on collective bargaining which came under severe strain in the 1960s, operated well in the 1970s but failed to avoid several major disputes in the 1980s. In the wake of the 1991 dispute, pluralist orthodoxy was being openly challenged and questioned, to the greatest extent by management, but by ESB unions as well.

British Liberal Pluralism and the Oxford School

The issue of public policy and trade unions had its first public airing in the 1867 Royal Commission on Trades Unions report, which marked the start of many formal inquiries into trade unions, industrial relations and reform. Founded in the aftermath of the secretary of the Sheffield Grinders Union placing gunpowder in the homes of "scab" workers, the Commission's work was more favourable to unions than expected. The question posed by the influential minority report has been asked and re-asked many times since: seeing that the bulk of the artisan population consider it in

their best interest to form themselves into these associations
(trade unions), in what way can they be rendered most conducive
to public policy? A later Royal Commission, the Royal Commission
on Labour, 1891-1894, put the essence of the relationship between
employer and employee more directly:

> Powerful trade unions on the one side and powerful associa-
> tions of employers on the other have been the means of bring-
> ing together in conference the representatives of both classes,
> enabling each to appreciate the position of the other and to un-
> derstand the conditions subject to which their joint undertak-
> ing must be conducted (Royal Commission on the Trades Un-
> ions and Employers' Associations, 1968: 12).

One hundred years after the Sheffield incidents, the Donovan
Commission reiterated what it saw as the best method for the
conduct of relations in the workplace (Royal Commission on the
Trades Unions and Employers' Associations, 1968: para 203):

> Collective bargaining is the best method of conducting indus-
> trial relations and there is therefore wide scope in Britain for
> extending both the subject matter of collective bargaining and
> the number of workers covered by such agreement.

This principle, and the reform of the legislation and practice that
has been built up around it, has dominated industrial relations
ever since.

Academic interest in industrial relations had developed
through the public policy commitment to collective bargaining as
the main vehicle of welfare and social control in industry, originat-
ing in the work of the Webbs (Webb and Webb, 1897). Pluralism as
a school of thought embodying collective bargaining developed
from two separate strands of thinking in America and the UK,
both of which sought to embrace the notion of change. While
American industrial relations theory was dominated by what became known as the "Harvard Berkeley Pluralist School", British
Liberal Pluralism developed around a group associated with the
Royal Commission. The Commission was set up in 1965 by the
then Prime Minister Harold Wilson and chaired by Lord Justice
Donovan after a period of major problems in British industrial
relations involving an outbreak of strikes, largely unofficial. A
similar committee set up by the Irish Government to look at the
rash of disputes in the ESB culminating in the 1968 strike
reached similar conclusions. The final report of the Fogarty

Committee, published in 1969, urged a strengthening of the Board's collective bargaining system, greater resources for unions and a firmer approach by management when faced by threats of power cuts. Both reports were a major influence on ESB industrial relations in the 1970s and 1980s and formed the basis of the management's approach until the late 1980s as we shall see later.

The immediate background to the Royal Commission was what was regarded as an intolerable volume of unofficial strikes in the 1960s, an inflationary pattern of competitive decentralised bargaining, pervasive restrictive practices, a deep-rooted resistance to change and a move in the post-war decades from industry to plant level bargaining. Outside mining, the number of disputes grew significantly with small scale unofficial actions in shipbuilding, the docks and the car industry receiving huge publicity. What were regarded as unofficial wildcat strikes had a major impact on public opinion. From the early to mid-1960s, the level of strike action had begun to rise in the public and private sectors and 90 per cent of the disputes were unofficial. The Commission, which included Hugh Clegg, and for which Alan Fox carried out major research, found that Britain had two systems of industrial relations. One was formal, embodied in official institutions while the other was informal, created by the actual behaviour of trades unions and employers, shop stewards and managers on the factory floor. It argued that the two systems were in conflict and that most of the strife in British industrial relations derived from this conflict. In his submission to the Commission in 1966, Alan Flanders criticised the "chaotic state of relations between managements and shop stewards" which he said resulted in:

> Unofficial strikes and earnings drift; in under-utilisation of labour and resistance to change; in the growth of systematic overtime and the demoralisation of incentive pay schemes; in inequitable and unstable factory pay structures and in a general decline in industrial discipline; in an undermining of external regulation by industry-wide and other agreements; and in a weakening of control by trade unions and employers' associations over their members (Clegg, 1990: 3).

This had led to an undermining of external regulation by industry-wide agreements and in a weakening of control by trade unions and employers associations over their members. The Commission recommended that the informal system of industrial relations, which had grown up through the post war decade in an uncodified, unplanned and uncoordinated way in an era of full employment, should be made formal. It also dealt with the problems of unions pushing up inflation through their organisational strength and the problem of low productivity growth. Among its central conclusions was that collective bargaining was the best and most democratic means of conducting industrial relations and that the role of law should be limited. It rejected various proposals for legal restraints to ban closed shops, to make agreements enforceable or to impose ballots or "cooling off periods".

In his Research Paper for the Royal Commission (1966), Alan Fox asked what sort of organisation is the industrial enterprise. Should it, or ought it, be analogous to a team unified by common purpose? Should it be viewed as a coalition of interests, a mini-democratic state composed of sections and groups with divergent interests over which the Government tries to maintain some kind of dynamic equilibrium? He ruled out the unitary system, whose principle feature is one source of authority and loyalty, and says that this has long since been abandoned by most social scientists as incongruent with reality. In place of a corporate unity reflected in a single focus of authority and loyalty he says that the existence of several rival sources of power should be accepted.

Critiques of Pluralist Reformism

A number of critics came to the fore in questioning some of the core values of the pluralist doctrine and chief among these writers were John Goldthorpe, Eric Batstone and David Metcalf. John Goldthorpe (1974: 419) restates the central tenets of the Oxford school of industrial relations which formed the bedrock of the Donovan report. The central view supported by the Oxford School, and generally regarded as the "liberal position", is that problems stem from the deficiencies and contradictions which have accumulated in the post-war period, particularly at workplace level. In many plants, bargaining was either highly fragmented or else effective control on the side of labour was in the hands of multi-union shops stewards committees, responsible to no one but themselves. The general effect was that of extensive breakdown in the normative regulation of industrial life or the creation of what Flanders and Fox referred to as a state of "anomie". Like Fox, Goldthorpe questioned the underlying assumptions of liberal pluralism and said that what in fact may be a problem with the system viewed from one perspective could be of no concern or even an advantage to others. He severely criticizes the depth of research carried out by the liberal reformers into workers themselves. In their major research on piece work, the liberal researchers interviewed management, foremen and union officials but not rank and file workers themselves. Thus proposals for formal company or plant agreements, whose absence was one of the keynotes of Donovan and which would bring full-time officials into a closer involvement with the affairs of the workplace, must be seen as threatening the autonomy of the shopfloor. He concludes that if the liberal programme for reform were to be realised, the consolidation of managerial capitalism would be the most likely outcome.

For Eric Batstone (1988: 120) industrial relations reform embodied two distinct strategies — procedural and substantive. The reformers' case as exemplified by Flanders was that their proposals meant the extension of union influence. In effect, plant and company agreements extended the range of issues negotiated between management and unions and the argument was that both would achieve greater control. But many of the radicals alleged that the procedural aspects of reform were aimed at reducing the power of shop stewards and that many of the substantive proposals were contrary to workers' interests. The reformist case was that union representatives would be involved in making the rules and thereby have wider influence. In return, management would have greater freedom in the day to day organisation of work. As a result fractitional bargaining would be reduced and shop floor-level negotiation would be structured by jointly agreed rules.

The logic of reform indicated a temporary increase in bargaining activity and a subsequent decline. But Batstone found that all the survey evidence suggested that reform led to an increase in the range and intensity of bargaining, and it did not appear to lead to a reduction in fractitional bargaining over job control issues.

Industrial relations reform was intended by Donovan to facilitate increased efficiency and productivity but it has been argued that the extent to which reform led to the greater managerial freedom in the use of labour is limited. Indeed, says Batstone, if anything its freedom to manoeuvre was reduced. Britain's slower rate of growth meant that by the mid-1970s, levels of real product per head were lower than in all main European countries. Batstone then sets out to look at the possible explanations for the poor British productivity record and to see what role industrial relations played in it. He also tries to forge a more direct link between the two.

If reform had been successful, then productivity should have grown more in those sectors where collective agreements were more common and where local agreements had been made, according to Batstone. But the results showed that the greater the coverage of collective agreements the lower the rate of productivity growth. If industrial relations reform was to be deemed successful, then the degree of worker control and influence over various aspects of their jobs should have been reduced as management gained greater freedom to deploy labour and increase effort. He concludes that reform did not lead to a reduction in shop floor bargaining, and when the increase in shop steward density is taken into account, it appears to have increased considerably. Reformism had not, however, militated against workers' interests and in fact they probably gained more than employers. This finding has a major bearing in the case of the ESB. Reform of the ground rules of collective bargaining, as epitomised in the Fogarty Report, ultimately worked in their favour.

David Metcalf (1989) notes that in the last 20 years there had been two types of attempts to reform industrial relations motivated by the desire to improve the competitive performance of the British economy, namely the Donovan strategy for the 1970s and the Thatcher strategy for the 1980s. Donovan put foward joint regulation to develop a more rational and coherent structure in industrial relations but, as Batstone pointed out above, fell down on the question of productivity and failed to match its own aspirations. Thatcher, on the other hand, took a more environmentalist strategy and emphasised market forces, the legislative framework and employee involvement. Before offering new insights on why Donovan-style reform failed, Metcalf notes that research reveals that the major institutions which were built around it are still largely intact. But much else has changed. In the 1980s, as compared with the previous decade, people are working harder, labour productivity is increasing, profits are up and strike activity is down. The Donovan reforms had failed to deliver on improving productivity. But by contrast, Thatcherism had, because it led to the fuller implementation of the original Donovan proposals to enhance productivity.

Human Resource Management (HRM) and Its Challenge to Pluralism

Richard E Walton (1985) argued that a broad consensus had emerged that US managers generally had come to rely upon poor models for managing their workforces, and ended up expecting much less from their workers than was potentially available. Building on the historical analysis of Paul Lawrence (1985), he identifies the emerging HRM system as the "commitment model". All its elements were aimed at eliciting commitment and he described the system which it was replacing as the "control model". The most dramatic evidence of US management's interest in developing new HRM models appeared in new plants built during the 1970s including plants of General Foods in Topeka, Kansas; General Motors at Brookhaven, Mississippi; Cummins Engines of Jamestown, New York and Proctor and Gamble at Lima, Ohio.

Walton, while admitting that there are many variations on the commitment model, outlines eight key features that make it unique. Job design policies result in teams rather than individuals being the unit accountable for performance, thus promoting mutuality at the level of task management. Performance expectations are set relatively high, emphasize improvements and are orientated to the marketplace but most of all are dynamic. Management hierarchies tend to be flat, relying upon shared goals and minimizing status differences. Compensation or pay policies reinforce group achievement, are more contingent on job definitions and are more complex, often offering a "menu" including gain sharing, stock ownership or profit sharing. In the employment assurance or job security area companies go to great lengths to avoid unemployment and retraining is a major component of policy. Increased employee voice, yielding greater mutual influence, is a central feature of the new management model and in the non-unionised setting a variety of mechanisms are used to inform staff. Labour-Management relations are meant to become less adversarial with a broadening of the relationship to include joint problem solving and planning but he sees this as a problem area of the new model. The management philosophy of the new model is often contained in a management "mission statement" outlining the multiple aims of the different stakeholders, employees, customers and the public. The fulfilment of employee needs is taken as a goal rather than merely as a means to other ends. The common thread of the policies of mutuality is first to elicit employee commitment and then to expect efficiency and effectiveness to follow as second

order consequences. Without mutual trust, management is forced
to re-institute controls to ensure acceptable performance.

Walton also puts forward a "transitional model" to aid the move
from existing control systems to the commitment system. This involved a limited set of work changes and the cornerstone of this
interim arrangement is involvement in problem solving groups in
the form of quality circles. Two approaches were outlined in the
theoretical literature on HRM: the integrated policy emphasis and
the corporate culture emphasis. The integrated approach highlights commitment arising from a set of interlinking policies such
as work organisation, pay and promotion and is deemed to be
more "hard nosed." This policy is designed to lead to a committed,
adaptive and flexible staff. The corporate culture approach involves the creation of "strong corporate cultures" and the management of symbols, values, and systems of value transmission. It
emphasizes stories, myths, rituals and corporate beliefs.

Union-Management Relations under HRM

Kochan, McKersie and Cappelli (1984) give five reasons for the
change from pluralist or control style models in American industrial relations that they believed were not adequately explained in
current theories. These include the decline in union membership
both in the non-agricultural and growth sectors of the American
economy which undermines the notion of collective bargaining as a
means of asserting their common interest. There have also been
changes in managerial values which make it more politically and
socially acceptable to embrace publicly a "union-free approach". In
recent years the decline in unionisation had also been accompanied by experiments in shop level participation including various
forms of worker participation. Increasingly management had been
taking the initiative in bargaining demands and in introducing
innovations into personnel practices in non-union employment.
Finally, there have also been changes in the role of Government.
Between 1960 and 1980 Government regulations concerning the
terms and conditions of employment expanded rapidly, but the
arrival of the Reagan administration resulted in a reversal of this
approach. The problems with the existing systems theory, as far
as Kochan et al are concerned, is that it fails to recognize that important decisions are taken at many other levels where shared
perspectives do not exist.

Trade Unionism and Human Resource Management: Are They Incompatible?

Terry Cradden (1992) tries to resolve the apparent contradictions between pluralism and HRM by pointing out that American studies have shown that the kind of "dual allegiance" which is the alternative to pure company or union loyalty is quite possible "where a co-operative industrial relations climate exists". The key to success, the author says, is an acknowledgement of the substantial value, in appropriate circumstances, of dual allegiance. What this requires of a union is that it identify closely with the production, quality and competitive aims of the employer and that it encourage the growth through participation of a greater sense of commitment on the part of its members to the organisation for which they work. On the management side it requires that they involve the union as well as individuals and work groups in all organisational decision-making, and just as important, in their implementation. Cradden gives some examples from the US where some companies started down the HRM style path with a strong union tradition. He instances Nissan, GM and Ford and the San Franciso Municipal Authority as a public service example.

Dualism and HRM

John Storey (1992) notes the extensive take up of HRM style approaches in the British mainstream organisations he studied. He measured the implementation of 25 key HRM variables in 15 major organisations including Austin Rover, British Rail, Ford, ICI, Jaguar and Lucas. But he pinpoints the lack of meshing and the room for improvement in the degree of cohesion between the initiatives undertaken under the HRM banner. In some cases, elements of the HRM plan were installed for a year, and 12 months later the attention moved to another key element. What emerges is that despite extensive engagement with large parts of HRM, Britain's large mainstream organisations have placed little emphasis upon abandoning their pluralist stance. What emerges is a duality of approach on the industrial relations scene. Trade union recognition and the appearances of collective bargaining were being maintained but running quite separately were a series of HRM initiatives. In some cases this "dual dealing", as Storey calls it, was even conducted by separate departments or units within the one firm and the communications between them was rudimentary and even hostile.

Transformation Disputes — Genesis and Aftermath

The concept "transformation disputes" is used here to denote disputes that involve major changes to the internal and external ground rules in an industry or a company, in the wake of traumatic disruptive action which challenges the prevailing industrial relations orthodoxy and groundrules. The very nature of the action and its impact or trauma on a community results in a break with the existing IR system and the assumptions which underpin it and how they are viewed by the major players. What gives such disputes their "transformative quality" are the changes in the regulatory, legislative or industry structure that may follow in their wake, usually implemented or initiated by Government. This may be mirrored by an attempt at internal industrial relations reform, sparked by the same set of dispute circumstances as the external change and geared at "getting the house in order". Our major concern here is with the impact of the explosive 1991 strike on management strategy, the challenge it posed to the conventional collective bargaining system and the opening it provided for Human Resource Management.

The roles of major strikes, such as the 1991 ESB dispute, in changing the ground rules for the conduct of relations with Government and between unions and managements has received little attention in the literature. One such transformative dispute was the 1985 British miners' strike which created conditions in which management were able to successfully undermine the power of the of the National Union of Mineworkers and gradually strip away and erode their bargaining power at local level. Whatever vestiges of union power remained were finally removed by a huge redundancy programme. The four month long dispute in TEAM Aer Lingus of summer 1994 also falls into the category of a transformation dispute

The Underpinnings of Pluralism and HRM

The rise of pluralism and of collective bargaining as a sustainable system of industrial relations was based firstly on the acceptance of its legitimacy by organised labour and business and by the political system, particularly the Government in power. Laws must be passed and rules adopted in industrial society and the best that could be expected was that they would emanate from a series of majorities (Kerr, 1964: 20). Not alone did it depend on substantial union density, which rose from 38 per cent to 45 per cent in the post war period, but on sustained economic growth and the development of mass production aimed at satisfying the needs of a growing mass market with a largely undifferentiated product range. Just as it adjusted to market demands and the need for greater productivity, pluralism's ability to sustain itself depended on the strength of collective bargaining to deliver mass products to a largely uniform market, at a rate which provided a return on capital and met prevailing wage demands.

The modern roots of pluralism as a method of industrial relations can be traced back to the economic, political and social environment of post-war Britain. In the United States, the rise and institutionalisation of collective bargaining can be traced to the New Deal and Keynesian economics.

The practice of industrial relations in Ireland has developed along pluralist lines with the establishment of the Labour Court in 1946 being a watershed. It encouraged the spread of collective bargaining in the private sector, dealing with recognition disputes at the same time as public service unions won negotiating rights in the Conciliation and Arbitration schemes. The level of trade union density attained by Irish unions increased from less than 20 per cent in the 1920s to a peak of over 60 per cent in 1980. Short- and medium-term fluctuations around this trend can be attributed to the business cycle and institutional influences on unionisation (Roche, 1992: 304). The development of pluralist industrial relations was in turn fostered and encouraged by State development agencies and went hand in hand with the professionalisation of the personnel function in both public and private sector management. By the late 1980s, however, many large organisations were exploring the basic concepts of human resource management, taking their cue in many cases from incoming US firms who had successfully managed a policy of union avoidance, particularly in the electronics industry.

No single causal explanation but rather a set of interdependent factors were responsible for the growing popularity of HRM concepts (Kochan, Katz and Mc Kersie, 1986: 51). In the United States management values towards unions evolved from encouragement to join the AFL-CIO affiliates in the 1950s in major industries to later support for independent unions. By the 1960s and 1970s this policy of mild encouragement had switched to a strategy of avoiding unions at all. Central to the decline of pluralism and its core values of adversarial bargaining and joint regulation was the new wave of competition, much of it from non-union firms, which were capable of responding to market demands and changing consumer tastes faster than their unionised counterparts. As competition increases the initial decision a firm must take is whether it wants to remain in that line of business and compete in the new changing circumstances or withdraw and pursue other opportunities.

The main industrial relations impact of an increased concern with prices and costs is that firms shift their priorities away from the maintenance of industrial peace to controlling their labour costs and streamlining their work rules, improving efficiency and promoting productivity. Changes in product market structure and in the intensity of competition also encourage firms to rearrange their capital, ultimately affecting the mix of job skills and work-force requirements. Another major reason for the decisions to move to new plants or to adopt union marginalisation policies in existing facilities was the economic incentive derived from the gap between the rates of union and non-union pay. By the 1970s, many firms were in a position to choose between investing in and ex-panding employment in a high cost union plant versus opening a new lower cost plant which could be operated on a non-union ba-sis. Wages in unionised plants were 10 to 15 per cent higher than in non-union facilities and by the 1970s few managers could find productivity gains to offset the up to 30 per cent total extra cost of the unionised fringe and pay packages. The change over to the more unitarist way of seeing the employee/manager relationship under HRM, designed ultimately to lead to a greater competitive advantage through a more committed staff, both mirrored and matched political developments in the UK and US. As Guest (1990) demonstrated, in the US the values associated with the new system — success through hard work and self improvement — fitted in with the persistent themes of the American Dream, in particular the "rugged individualism" stereotype.

Much of the writing on management strategy does not distin-guish between the problems of reform in the public and private sectors. There are valid reasons why the process and problems of reform vary from one sector to the other. Ownership and the in-terplay between Government and management can shape and condition union management relations in the public sector and this has implications for both reform and the smooth conduct of relations.

State Control in Public Enterprise

According to Ferner (1988: 29), the defining characteristic of public State enterprises is that they are subject to some form of political control. The ESB was created by the Electricity (Supply) Act 1927 and many of its early goals involved meeting political as well as economic targets. The areas of activity of State enterprises are defined by politicians. They are given objectives, constraints are imposed on them and their performance is monitored. In this way they are led to pursue goals which would not be achieved by leaving the activity to the private enterprise sector. The victory of the Conservatives in the British general election of 1979 led to a radical questioning of the role of the public enterprise sector which later resulted in a move to reduce the weight of the State in economic activity. State firms may frequently be asked to accept a role in maintaining employment to preserve political accommodations. The objectives of public enterprises mirror the complexity of the role of the State itself. This applies in the Irish Midlands where ESB is obligated to run high cost turf burning stations that produce electricity at largely uneconomic rates to maintain jobs, which as we shall see later produced its own type of political exchange at local level.

The major formal sanction in the hands of Governments is the power of appointment and dismissal over Boards and normally chief executives of public enterprises. Ferner (1988: 44) holds that State enterprises operate in an environment in which corporate objectives are subject to continuous renegotiation and intervention by fragmented political authorities. In the Irish context this applies in areas such as investment decisions, industrial relations issues including pay determination and restructuring and rationalisation plans. Thus the Government does not merely confine itself to setting the "rules of the game" but is in a sense a participant in industrial relations to the extent that it wants to intervene. The management of the state enterprise ceases to be the unions' sole potential bargaining partner. As a result, formal or informal bargaining may take place across the boundaries of the corporation between unions and political authorities, ministers, governments and local or regional authorities. Government intervention on pay, by putting pressure on the management to settle or even funding additional increases, encourages the unions to deal with "the organ grinder, not the monkey".

Political Exchange

The bargaining relations between State enterprise unions and the political authorities may be seen in terms of Pizzorno's well known concept of political exchange (Pizzorno 1978: 278). In the labour market, the commodity being sold is labour power; in the political market, the union is trading on the power to prevent disruption. In Pizzorno's words the actor, generally the Government, which has goods to give is ready to trade them in exchange for social consensus with an opposing actor who can threaten to withdraw it. A spin-off from the orientation of state enterprise unions to the political sphere is that industrial disputes or strikes may be aimed at putting political pressure on Government as much as economic pressure on the company's management. It may mean that strikes are openly directed against state policy as much as against management's negotiating position. Ferner (1988: 45) describes the complex relations that can occur by saying:

> The scope for political exchange complicates the nature of bargaining in state enterprise industrial relations. In addition to the conventional bilateral union-management negotiations of the private sector both parties may be engaged in simultaneous bilateral negotiations with the political authorities.

This might be called "triangular" bargaining negotiations in which each of the parties deals bilaterally with the other two. At times triangular bargaining may be supplemented by "tripartite" bargaining, that is, where the three parties negotiate jointly. In effect, the unions have another bargaining partner: not only does Government set the rules of the game but it may join it through occasional intervention. Unlike the labour market, what is being traded is power to prevent disruption of services or of an industry, and the agreements are tacit understandings, informal and usually unwritten. Much of the thinking and practice in Irish Civil Service industrial relations machinery, the Conciliation and Arbitration Scheme, is based on the same "exchange" principle. Strike action is not permitted in return for "special" or catch up pay awards paid at specific intervals. The "political" nature of the exchange is given its most concrete expression by the unique proviso that such special pay awards can only be overturned by a vote of the Irish parliament.

Political exchange has been a significant feature of ESB industrial relations. It also featured in many of the disputes considered in Chapter One — Irish Steel, TEAM and Aer Lingus, in particular. The ESB's collective bargaining machinery was created in 1969 out of a compromise between unions and Government, in the face of a strike threat. Ministerial intervention between the political authorities and ESB management and unions led to the resolution of the April 1991 dispute. And efforts at reform were also hampered by political intervention which ultimately underpined the highly internalised Joint Industrial Council system. The eventual threat of externally imposed change to the ESB's structure and its bargaining practices were, however, to have a more lasting impact.

Chapter Four

THE RISE OF PLURALISM IN THE ESB

Introduction

Chapter One outlined the way in which collective bargaining arrangements in six of Ireland's leading semi-state companies reached breaking point under the combined pressures of increasing competition, European deregulation and increased Government demands for commercialisation in the early 1990s. The dominant post-war model of industrial relations, known in the academic literature as the "pluralist model", which envisaged strong unions and professional managers, has held an unassailable position in the semi-state sector up to very recently. The refined bargaining system created in the ESB in the early 1970s represented an elaborate pluralist initiative. This "state of the art" model had much in common with arrangements in other semi-state companies, which, as we have seen earlier, is now subject to serious questioning by unions, managements and Governments. The system was seen to work well in the 1970s, a period of significant employment growth and less restrictive pay policy, but faced major difficulties in the 1980s, an era of a plateauing electricity demand.

Developments in ESB industrial relations in the 1980s highlight a system which had increasing difficulty coping with more commercial demands made on it, eventually resulting in serious management disillusionment with the key bargaining institutions. The inability to deliver change led to a toughening of management approach and a shift, partly influenced by European developments, to a more flexible human resource model, which will be considered in detail in the next chapter. Developments in the ESB in the 1980s mirror difficulty in dispute resolution in a number of other semi-state companies.

This chapter will demonstrate how the development of bargaining in the ESB approximated to pluralist ideals outlined by the major writers, in particular through the Donovan-style reforms introduced by the Fogarty Committee in 1969. As well as outlining the high points of liberal pluralism through the reasonably posi-

tive relations of the 1970s and early 1980s, it seeks to draw out
management's growing disillusionment with the system as it operated and the system's growing strains and contradictions. The
crisis in pluralist relations from the mid-1980s, best represented
by management's "no give policy" and the referral of all major issues to the Joint Industrial Council, are explored as key elements
of the failure to reform.

The background to the shattering ESB dispute of April 1991
and the policy shift it engendered can best be understood by examining the development of industrial relations strategy within the
company since its creation in 1927, as the first Irish public enterprise, committed to electrifying the homes and businesses of the
emerging State. As demand increased and additional staff were
taken on, the importance of industrial relations within the company increased and greater specialisation followed as responsibility was moved from Board members to an emerging personnel department.

The development of collective bargaining and the later
strengthening of the pluralistic model by the template outlined by
the Fogarty Committee in 1969, all provide a backdrop to the
hard-edged policy that was to dominate the 1980s: a period of low
growth and major external pressure on prices. This hardening of
approach, generally perceived to have occurred in the post-1983
period, forms the immediate historical background to the ground
breaking week-long strike of April 1991. The strike, which received an unprecedented level of support from groups not generally disposed to the electricians at the centre of the row, resulted
in the longest power cuts in the Board's recent history, created a
huge public outcry and put the entire operations of the Board under the public microscope as well as seriously undermining management confidence. It also led to a reappraisal at Government
level on the desirability of vesting the entire national generating
capacity in one company and an erosion in ministerial support.
Major figures on the union and management sides in the Board
are now convinced that the high level of support the strike secured
was the expression of staff reaction to the tougher management
stance of the preceding eight years and to their policy of resisting
claims.

General Background

The ESB, established in 1927 under the Electricity (Supply) Act, was one of the first State-sponsored bodies to be set up in Ireland. It has a virtual monopoly of the supply, distribution and production of electricity in the Republic of Ireland and purchases its own fuels as well as selling appliances and installation services to business and domestic customers. It was founded by the Government in a country that was just five years independent and its creation was a recognition by ministers of the time that the electrification of the country was the most vital ingredient for national economic and social reconstruction. The minister responsible for sponsoring the vesting legislation, Patrick McGilligan, was to say later that he was convinced from his observation of other countries that electricity was "too important a service in society to be left to privately owned companies whose objective was the accumulation of profit" (Moriarty: 1990). Its general duties under the initial act were to operate manage and maintain the Shannon scheme and to distribute and sell its output; to promote and encourage the purchase of electricity and to control, co-ordinate and improve the supply, distribution and sale of electricity.

Staffing and Structure

As one of the largest employers in the country with over 10,000 people on the payroll, the ESB plays a pivotal role in the Irish economy, not alone in terms of employment but also as a provider of the main source of power to both industrial and domestic users based on its role as a monopoly provider. Its size, influence and role, therefore, mean that the conduct of industrial relations in the Board assume a much greater importance than they would in other businesses of similar or lesser size in either the public or private sectors. Of the ESB's 10,000 staff, roughly 5,500 are concentrated in its six distribution regions and are responsible for the construction and maintenance of networks as well as revenue collection and customer services. About 3,000 staff are employed in generation. Management of the Board's 20 electricity producing stations is decentralised with each unit having its own manager and local headquarters. Figure 3.1 illustrates the growth in staff numbers in the Board since 1931 which peaked in the early 1980s at slightly over 13,000. Prior to 1984 there were four generating regions. Now, however, the stations are grouped according to the fuel source used such as coal/oil/gas, hydro/milled peat and sod peat. These changes were brought about on foot of the recommendations contained in the Miller Barry report (1984).

FIGURE 3.1:
ESB EMPLOYMENT LEVELS 1931-93

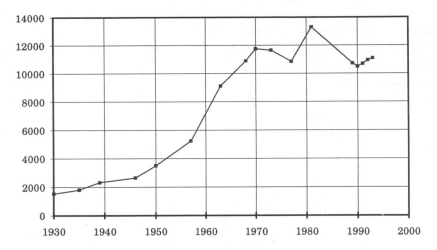

Source: Manning and McDowell, 1984; *ESB Annual Reports*.

Under the McKinsey restructuring proposals accepted by the Board in 1993, the ESB was divided into five separate business units responsible for generation, transmission systems, customer services, ancillary services and a central business service unit. Five managing directors were appointed to head each of the divisions in July 1993. Three Corporate Directors were appointed with responsibility for corporate strategy, technology, finance and personnel and to assist the Chief Executive in the formulation of policy. Formerly nine Executive Directors held responsibility for the key areas.

Evolution of Industrial Relations

In the early years of the ESB the company was small enough for the problems of individual employees to be dealt with at Board level. At first things were done on an "ad hoc" basis and the beginnings of a personnel policy are to be found in the establishment in 1935 of a staff section in the Board's administration area. Two Tribunals were set up to deal with employee issues during the 1940s, the first of these being the Manual Workers Tribunal established under the ESB (Superannuation) Act of 1942 which was created to deal with, among other things, how a strike would affect pension calculations. After a series of disputes around 1948 the Government in the following year set up a Tribunal to deal with the concerns of white collar or general workers, many of whom were not formerly unionised.

Between 1927 and 1960, or during the first 33 years of its existence, the Board experienced a mere eight strikes, six official and two unofficial — none of which seriously threatened supply. Between 1961 and 1968 the number of strikes jumped to 38 — 11 of which were official.

However, even in advance of the Fogarty Committee beginning its investigations, the Government had decided that the arbitration system in the Board would have to change. In February 1966 it announced that the two existing Tribunals, catering for manual and non-manual workers, which had been established in 1946 and 1949, should be abolished. The Labour Court later brought forward proposals which were agreed by both sides to establish a single arbitration body in the form of a Joint Industrial Council (JIC) but only after the unions had threatened industrial action. As Manning and McDowell point out (1984: 201):

> The Bill giving effect to the Government proposal to abolish the Tribunals was introduced into the Dáil in April 1966, but was not finally passed into law until June 1969. In the meantime, protracted negotiations took place between the ESB and the unions and the staff associations. In the course of these negotiations, initial reluctance by the unions and associations to abandon separate arbitration procedures was a major difficulty. Discussions on union and ESB proposals continued through 1967, 1968 and the first half of 1969. At this stage the passage of the bill into law brought matters to a head, with union representatives indicating some form of industrial action would be contemplated if the Government proposals to abolish the tribunals was implemented without a satisfactory replacement.

The political origins of the Joint Industrial Council, it will be argued later, partly contributed to the difficulty in bargaining relations in the 1980s and particularly the unions' reluctance to reform it. Final agreement on the JIC proposal was later reached in February 1970. This agreement provided for the setting up of the Joint Industrial Council with an independent chairman and permanent representatives of staff and management. During particular disputes two additional members would join the council, one on either side.

The Fogarty Report

The *Final Report of the Committee on Industrial Relations in the Electricity Supply Board* (ESB) published in March 1969 constitutes the most detailed in depth study into the background to the rash of disputes that broke out in the Board in the 1960s and of the weaknesses in the system of collective bargaining that had operated in the Board up to that time. The Committee found and agreed with the view of the ESB management at the time that there was a serious problem of "inefficient and fragmented representation of electricity supply workers in both manual and white collar grades" (*Final Report of the Committee on Industrial Relations in the ESB*, 1969: 28). Each category of the ESB's employees should be represented by one "most representative" union and each union group should have a clear cut constitution and rules reflecting the best trade union practice. The Committee also restated its position outlined in the interim report about the multiplicity of unions leading to waste and inefficiency. Overall, the three man Fogarty Committee found that the unions in the ESB were not equipped to think ahead, or head off new problems before they arose, or reform their own structures or procedures in time to meet new circumstances. It found a "dangerous complacency" on the sides of both the ESB and its unions.

On the management side the Committee recommended more attention be paid to advance thinking, quicker and more thorough handling of minor industrial relations issues and the hiring of personnel specialists as well as the improvement of staffing of the Personnel Department. It also recommended the strengthening of the personnel function in the ESB, new machinery for the conduct of collective bargaining and the possibility of increasing the delegation of authority in personnel matters to local level and to district, regional and station managers. More attention needed to be paid to long range strategy. Better internal and external communication was also advocated and where unions failed to communicate their members' views to the ESB, the company should step in itself to do the job. The personnel officer was to be renamed chief personnel officer and be given the same status as the other chief officers in the Board. More attention needed to be paid to advance thinking and long-term strategy and the strengthening of the personal element in leadership at the top executive positions. Better internal communication was also urged with provision for management meetings and conferences. Attention was also to be given to district and station managers' techniques for communications downwards. In addition, a joint procedure for regularly taking the industrial relations temperature of the organisation through attitude surveys and opinion polls was also suggested.

The first Director of Personnel was appointed in 1970 and, taking account of the recommendations of Fogarty, major emphasis was placed on the development of a personnel policy which would be derived from and supportive of the corporate objective of the ESB. The first comprehensive agreement was signed with the unions in 1971. A new and senior position of manager, industrial relations was later created and supported by a team of officers and back-up staff. According to Canning (1981: 102):

> In the early 1970s there was a crusading spirit in the ESB in the field of industrial relations, with a will to generate improvements and a committed organisation to back it up. Instead of reacting to developments, initiatives were taken by management at every level: at local level through improved negotiating procedures and a fresh approach to joint consultation, and at central level through more effective planning and organisation.

The 1980s: Redefining Personnel Policy, the "Claims Culture" and the Emerging Harder Industrial Relations Model

The quickening pace of industrial action in the late 1970s, including the working to rule by staff in 1977 over a new productivity deal and the Poolbeg dispute in 1979, led to a new Personnel Policy being issued by the new Director of Personnel in July 1980. The new policy took note of the events in the intervening seven years since the previous policy was published and highlighted the "growing resort to the chain of institutions and honest brokers" outside the workplace. The exploitation of change and the emergence of the State as a bargaining partner were cited as national problems faced by the Board which had been confronted with "increased industrial unrest and consequential closures". It highlighted the situation in the general economy the Board had to cope with: double digit inflation and high interest rates, as well as the cost of introducing social legislation (Fahy: 1980). The new personnel policy, while utilising many of the same section headings as its 1973 predecessor like "open society" and "social responsiveness", dropped many of its loftier ambitions and was much more geared to meeting day-to-day problems and less concerned with a long-term vision and the fostering of mutual trust. It attempted to re-present some of the earlier personnel and Fogarty concepts, but in the context of the hard-learned experience of the intervening years. In effect, it provided a harder edge to the existing policy and placed greater emphasis on the external environment facing the Board.

Looking back over the period since the Fogarty rules were introduced, one senior figure who played a central role summed up how he felt the system had operated:

> Up to 1981 it worked well, a lot of the old issues had been cleared and there was money. Between 1970 and 1980 most of the big deals were done. We bought our way out of problems. It was not a different attitude, it was money, with the company saying we will buy this and do that.

This had resulted in a situation where:

> Money washed away issues but gave rise to a culture that deals could be done and things could be bought. We have moved away from this to an extent. In those days you had large settlements and got little back. The next stage was where you got moderate settlements and a bit more back. Now everyone accepts that you get nothing for nothing.

Many saw the 1970s as a move away from old style autocratic management. In the 1980s, when firmer bargaining for money emerged, some managers reverted to a confrontational approach rather than a participative one. The whole notion of participation had taken on very slowly. In the opinion of a senior figure close to the situation on the company side, this was more of a reluctance of management to communicate rather than an unwillingness by trade unions to take part:

> The good managers were skilled enough to be able to do it very well while other managers, who were not skilled at interpersonal skills and regarded themselves as bosses, did not try to communicate information. We started briefing groups so that people would know what was going on. A lot of managers want to be seen as the boss who gives the orders and the instructions. And I think that within the ESB still there is a very large culture of autocracy in the way they work.

In order to rationalise the whole pay area, stem the flow of category claims and avoid demarcation disputes, the Board reached agreement with the trade unions for a new comprehensive agreement in 1981 which provided generous payments of 15 per cent over three years in addition to a lead-in lump sum of four weeks' pay. The objectives of the agreement were threefold: to have industrial peace in the ESB, to facilitate the orderly introduction of change and to maintain the levels of pay and conditions that reflected the high standard of performance and commitment by ESB staff to customer service in accordance with the Personnel Policy document of July 1980. In addition to the pay rises provided for, which were separate to national agreements, staff received £75 worth of free electricity in what was a costly but ultimately effective deal. The economy, however, was booming, electricity growth had risen to eight per cent and staff numbers were at an all-time high of 13,301. But the underlying trends told a different story. In the decade 1972-82 sales increased by 52 per cent, customers by 30 per cent and units sold by staff by 28 per cent. Payroll costs per employee had risen by 46 per cent while the rise in units sold was 28 per cent or nine per cent in relation to the number of customers which was regarded as a poor productivity performance. As a result, the Chief Executive was told that these trends, unless reversed, offered little encouragement towards his objective of keeping electricity prices below the national inflation rate.

The 1981 deal, which refocussed attention on procedures, effectively strengthening them through the introduction of penalties for non-delivery of industrial peace, was, however, built on over-optimistic predictions of growth in demand. Its operation would seem to confirm the view that pluralism functions best during boom periods when it delivers the optimum returns to the workforce. In this sense the 1981 agreement can be seen as "the last throw of the dice" or final attempt to implement the Fogarty proposals on their own terms or in the original spirit of the 1969 report. This is not to suggest that after the three-year deal expired in 1984 senior management jettisoned the basic framework Fogarty proposed — rather that they operated it in a more hard-headed way under the twin external pressures of low growth and growing public concern over its price structure. The new agreement itself came under strain from a strike in Poolbeg Station in January 1982 over the appointment of a shift relief supervisor from an outside station in Rhode, County Offaly, which had been opposed by the unions.

Procedure versus Culture

In response to management criticisms of the industrial relations

procedures at the time and their value in a climate of change, a
review of IR procedures in the Board was initiated in November
1983 by the Deputy Manager of the IR Department. The eight-
man ESB review group, with executives from all sectors of the
company represented, was to throw up a wide array of views on
the problems of winning change with the greatest frustration and
soul-searching evident among those charged with responsibility
for generation. It concluded that the existing industrial relations
procedures were, viewed objectively, "fundamentally sound". Any
perceived shortcomings were not enough to account for the high
incidence of claims, resistance to change and the increasing frus-
trations in taking any issue to finality through negotiations. Instead it found:

> It is attitudes which contribute to the manipulation of proce-
> dure and unless attitudes are right there can be no confidence
> that revised procedures will be any more than cosmetic and any
> less subject to manipulation. There has to be a fundamental
> appraisal of attitudes and expectations in the ESB and an ad-
> justment of policies and practices so as to generate the cultural
> change necessary for the conditions of the 1980s.

The full report of the committee painted a picture of an industrial
relations system, locally and centrally, which was "chronically
overloaded" with a case load of about 400 disputes in various
stages of negotiation. It noted that many managers considered
there was an over-emphasis on procedural considerations at the
expense of commercial reality, and that the growing trend towards
manipulation of the procedures indicated a deliberate strategy on
the part of the unions to maximise the pay-off to them either in
terms of benefits won or changes delayed. What was needed was a
means of ensuring that the large volume of industrial relations
business was reduced to more realistic and manageable proportions, and that the genuine necessities of the business to develop
and adapt were facilitated in a more commercially acceptable way.
But where stood the Fogarty proposals and the personnel policy in
all of this? The review believed that the findings of Fogarty:

> Generated a reforming attitude towards ESB personnel man-
> agement which though necessary in its time, has given rise to a
> culture and a constitutional position which the organisation
> seems to have to defend whether it has the money or not.

If this was the case it was naive to blame the unions for intransi-
gence since they had everything to gain by exploring each and

every avenue of the procedural labyrinth. In the end the review
concluded that:

> A combination of protective staff policies, absence of clear eco-
> nomic definition, a generally tolerant management attitude
> bordering on resignation and the diffuse accountability for the
> cost of delays sustain a culture which tolerates the exploitation
> of industrial relations procedures.

Against this background of "bad faith" in the existing IR system,
and after advocating the primacy of a cultural solution to dealing
with the flood of claims, the committee went on to make six recommendations for the effective tightening of claims procedure. Ill-
founded claims were to be stifled at local level, fewer meetings
with unions were advocated, claims were to go from local un-
ion/management level to arbitration and the ESB's policy of accepting all Industrial Council recommendations was to be kept
under review. Implicit in the review document, but not stated, was
the message that the personnel policy of the 1970s had failed to
deliver a culture of trust and openness which could deal and respond to problems caused by the external environment as they
emerged. Many of the submissions to the review advocated major
changes in procedure such as a two-tier Joint Industrial Council,
settling more cases outside the council and a reduction in the
number of meetings at central level. A change in the company's
"no give" policy was also advocated. Many executives could simply
not understand why staff they regarded as having good working
conditions produced such a multiplicity of claims. The feeling of
despair shared by many executives arising from being trapped in a
constitutional system they felt did not work satisfactorily was best
summed up by one generation executive. His thesis was that while
the procedures would continue to give industrial peace at the price
of "organisational stagnation and increasing inefficiency" they
would not deliver change without an appropriate alteration in the
environment. He believed the ESB was "snookered" by a veto of
"the managed on the proposals of the managers". As a result there
was no way out other than to examine the ideologies of the left and
to see to what extent they could accommodate them to achieve
movement. Another Board executive felt that the system itself was
at fault:

> It is very difficult to concentrate people's minds on reaching a
> solution in direct negotiations because everyone feels, both now
> and then that serious issues are not going to be reached across

the table. No matter what you say or what you do there is another wind in the process of going to the industrial council. People reserve their best ammunition for the Council because they know they are going to go there. That is one of the biggest problems we have had all the time and that we had with the TEEU.

One union leader with extensive experience of the ESB pinpoints this period as the time when management set out to marginalise the unions. Rather than being driven by any particular policy, they were influenced by the prevailing tougher political mood evident in the treatment of unions, particularly in the UK:

There was one strategy and that was do not deal with unions. But there were some good managers. There were some managers who could bury things away from head office and there was winking and nudging and there was trust and it worked. I did not know about it and the management did not know but the business was done.

A leading figure on the management side at the time concurs with the view of the pervasive political mood having a major impact on how ESB managers saw themselves:

The 1980s were an era of recession; in the 1970s there was a shortage of people and staff felt confident. We were into the era of Thatcherism in the UK when the unions were being bashed but Irish management and ESB management said that we should be doing this too and we should put manners on them. There was a bad attitude until the Programme for National Recovery in 1987. That was the first clear signal it was not Government's intention to marginalise the unions. It was not official policy in the ESB but I think individual managers sought to relegate the trade unions to a less powerful role.

The absence of competition and the fact that the ESB is a monopoly producer of electricity is cited by senior management who were strongly supportive of the Personnel Policy at the time as a major barrier to change.

External Pressure and Pushing through Miller Barry

Buffeted by criticism of its price levels and with a 10 per cent rise in tariffs being considered by Government, the Chief Executive of the ESB in July 1983 put forward proposals for a five-year strategic plan covering the period up to 1988. Under it, an ESB Task Force was set up to work with consultants Miller Barry to "review the structures, authorities and relationships appropriate to the eighties and in line with good electricity utility practice in other countries". The background to the plan was that the Board saw itself in an era of much reduced activity with all its major infrastructure complete. The outlook for electricity growth for the decade was low, with growth of three to five per cent predicted. The organisation was top heavy with overheads and electricity prices were seen to be too high. The Board still believed itself to be overstaffed as it moved from a high growth expansionist era into a period of low growth. In fact, the issue of overstaffing compared to other electricity utilities abroad was an issue of embarrassment for the Chief Executive; when he travelled to Denmark and was exposed to constant questioning having to disclose ESB staffing levels according to one file. The organisational structure varied from 13 to 50 years in age, only one of the 12 districts had shown a profit in the year to March 1985 and some of the structures were not seen as appropriate to the challenge ahead. The reorganisation plan involved achievement of reductions in management positions of the order of 25 per cent in head office, the replacement of the 12 administrative districts by six regions with the personnel function being decentralised. The unions declined to co-operate with the review and when the final proposals for reorganisation were to emerge they resulted in major conflict with management, particularly on the issue of consultation and negotiation on many of its key elements. The official ESB position was that it was prepared to negotiate on all aspects of the joint ESB consultants' report to get agreement as early as possible.

The Chief Executive made clear that it was for the management appointed by the Board to determine how to organise the activities under them and to communicate, consult and negotiate with staff as appropriate about these matters. Guarantees were given that no one would lose his or her employment or be forced to relocate family or home. To the unions, however, this amounted to not having any legitimate negotiating rights in respect of organisational structure or implementation timescale. The handling of Miller Barry internally was regarded as part of a new and tougher management policy, partly influenced by the need to reduce costs and overheads without incurring significant expenditure.

During the 1980s, however, for the first time in its history the Board faced a static or falling demand for electricity at a time when its pricing policy was coming under severe external criti-

cism. Table 4.1 shows that while the average price per unit of electricity sold almost doubled between 1979/80 and 1985/86, the
number of customers was static. Public attacks on the Board to
the effect that it was overstaffed increased and this view was later
confirmed by the company itself. In fact, Sweeney (1990) cites the
Jakobsen report into prices in the ESB published in 1984 which
said that there were 4,000 too many people employed at that time
but it provided no basis for the assertion. The ESB a year later
said that the figure was closer to 2,000 at a cost of £34 million
(Sweeney, 1990: 137). And the *Joint Oireachtas Report on Semi-
State Bodies* (1986: 67) said that the general consensus was that
the ESB was still significantly overmanned by comparison with
other utilities and it put the figure as high as 2,000. In the 1980s
numbers had been reduced from a peak of 13,301 in 1981/82 to
10,724 in 1989. In 1984 the ESB introduced a voluntary early re-
tirement/redundancy scheme and numbers have declined since
then. The 1993 annual report records that 11,093 people are employed overall by the ESB, 10,028 of whom are engaged in electricity supply.

TABLE 4.1:
GROWTH OF ESB 1930-93

Year	Units Generated and Purchased (millions)	Units Sold to Customers (millions)	Revenue from Electricity Sales (£)	Average Price per Unit Sold (pence)	Customers
1929/30	60.9	43.2	478	1.108	48,606
1939/40	407.0	318.6	1,946	0.612	172,545
1949/50	784.8	626.1	4,774	0.763	310,639
1959/60	2,096.0	1,692.2	14,724	0.871	610,947
1969/70	5,245.7	4,411.6	39,400	0.892	786,500
1979/80	10,231.6	8,560.3	300,024	3.505	1,043,428
1985/86	11,465.1	9,787.8	757,172	7.736	1,194,765
1990	13,895.4	11,768.0	756,074	6.425	1,278,870
1991	14,634.6	12,370.1	785,205	6.348	1,302,061
1992	15,470.6	13,103.9	826,464	6.307	1,326,547
1993	---	13,438.7	842,416	6.269	1,348,196

Source: ESB Annual Reports, 1992, 1993.

Harsher economic realities in the early 1980s, a less benign political environment and excess capacity led to a view being developed in the Board that the consensual approach enshrined by the 1970s productivity agreements had not delivered the major changes which had been sought. Canning (1981: 106) said that the environmental factors in the 1970s manifested themselves in category and relativity consciousness, suspicion of change and the notion that "everything should be negotiable in terms of a price tag".

By 1984 Miller Barry consultants noted the need to reduce overhead costs, for more rigorous business planning and the necessity to give priority to improving standards of customer service. Because of the high price of electricity and other factors such as its high borrowings and accumulated deficits, the consultants concluded that the ESB found itself "perhaps unreasonably facing reduced confidence by the Government and the customer community" (Miller Barry, 1984: 1-2). Since the last major reorganisation in 1970 the numbers of head office staff had increased by 47 per cent while in the same period numbers in the rest of the ESB had increased by only 10 per cent. It urged a greater emphasis on employee relations as opposed to industrial relations, the maintenance of positive relations with employees and trade unions and the implementation throughout the ESB of co-operative structures. In addition, it proposed that the Personnel Organisation should be restructured. Personnel functions were to be decentralised. Miller Barry (4-60) state that they believed that one of the reasons for the large number of claims was the relative brevity with which labour contracts were written. Central processing of claims also led to excessive cost and lost time. Lack of management/union consultative structures had led to a consequent over-emphasis on adversarial collective bargaining.

Many of the 1980s disputes were linked to the decline in demand for electricity and the reorganisation that followed it. A dispute in 1984 centred on crucial aspects of a £7 million job shedding plan, where unions took the view that management was out to crush them. The row centred on transferring staff from Ringsend Power Station, which had employed 230 and was out of the system, and Poolbeg where there were some vacancies but people were earning high overtime. A pay dispute in May 1987 saw the Government taking a tough stance behind the ESB when the unions found themselves in the position of being pay leaders on the battlefield of the 26th pay round.

The May 1987 Dispute Over the 26th Pay Round

A pay dispute over the 26th pay round in May 1987 saw the management firmly holding its ground despite power cuts resulting from three days of strike action by all staff, with the exception of engineers and some managers, over a 10 per cent pay claim. The Joint Industrial Council had recommended a rise averaging three and a half per cent after a three month pay pause and this was accepted by the Board. The dispute was resolved on May 7 during intensive negotiations that the Minister for Labour helped to arrange. The settlement provided for the unions accepting an already rejected Industrial Council recommendation, a formula for the conclusions of negotiations on other issues and a peace clause which required adherence to agreed procedures in all future disputes. Discount vouchers for ESB employees worth between £150 and £250 were also included. It also allowed for the speedy implementation of change and of another previously rejected Industrial Council recommendation on free electricity.

Within the Board the settlement was seen as vindicating the firm stance taken by the ESB to what they regarded as "extreme trade union pressure". The settlement was seen by the ESB as having lasting implications way beyond the strike. In particular, clause two of the agreement, which provided that the ESB unions "give a solemn joint commitment to the peaceful and speedy implementation of changes in systems, procedures, work methods and equipment in the interests of promoting the best modern electricity utility standards", was seen as a breakthrough. Clause one of the deal allowed that negotiations would be concluded through procedures or the Joint Industrial Council on the "understanding that the outcome of each claim will produce economies that will benefit the consumer". While the row was ostensibly about pay, more seasoned observers saw it as a "flexing of union muscle". The outcome was seen as a boost to Government efforts to contain the escalating public pay bill.

Reforming the Joint Industrial Council

During discussions on proposed amendments to the agreement for the Joint Industrial Council the management rejected suggestions that it wanted the Council to "die on the vine". It put forward two sets of proposals for reform, one of which included binding arbitration. The manager of employee relations argued that there had been "loss of confidence in direct negotiations" leading to chronic overloading of the Council. This in turn had resulted in a loss of

confidence in the Council which had affected attitudes towards it
and its recommendations. He pointed out:

> I am convinced that the root of the problem lies in what I have
> described as the "Council mentality" i.e. that the Council is
> built into everyone's thought processes during negotiations and
> claimants have no incentive to settle or withdraw because ex-
> perience shows that there is nothing to lose by heading to the
> Council.

If the Council was to be preserved it needed to be reformed so that
it became less predictable to the parties, with both sides being
obliged to weigh up more carefully the possibility of losing at
Council level before direct negotiations were concluded. Later, the
ESB accepted "reluctantly" that the unions were not ready for the
kind of change which was needed in the operation of the Council to
meet modern needs. Significantly, it was the Government, in the
form of the Department of Finance, that expressed concern at the
prospect of an agreement on binding arbitration anywhere in the
public service. However, provision was made for "pendulum" adjudication where there was a request from both parties. At one
stage the management considered serving the unions with six
months notice of withdrawal in the context of setting up a joint
working party to recommend new machinery. But this was seen as
a major propaganda opportunity for the unions. In the end the
Council remained substantially the same; the unions agreed to
pay travelling expenses for staff travelling to hearings and the
other changes were minor technical ones. But from about 1988 on,
after an explosive rise in claims, the Council was to adopt a more
rigorous approach, insisting that local negotiations take place between the parties before cases were lodged. The current chairman
of the Council is known to be sympathetic to the view that it
should function in a two-tier fashion; a formal conciliation process
would precede cases going to full Council, effectively making it a
"court of last resort".

The then Board view of the JIC is summed up by one executive
with detailed knowledge of its workings:

> By the mid-1980s we had all become too comfortable and cosy
> with the situation and we had to change it. We were still doing
> the same things and the chairman had become somewhat pre-
> dictable. He gave the principle to the company and the money
> to the unions. They got so used to getting the money, it became
> intolerable.

However, when the Board had signalled they wanted to change the structure "the warning bells" rang and opposition to change strengthened. The JIC is regarded by senior people in the company as "too much part of 1970s ESB culture". A proposal emerged on one occasion to reject a JIC recommendation in a case that carried little potential risk of disruption as a symbol of management's independence. But this was rejected by the Chief Executive. Accepting council recommendations provides management with a certain moral authority when it came to dealing with its outcomes over any period of time. But the "soft touch factor" and the fact that the council is not subject to the financial pressures the Board faces has made executives less than totally supportive of its structure.

As far back as 1979 the then Assistant Chief Executive questioned the value of renewing its mandate expressing a preference for the more public forum of the Labour Court. This was to emerge again very clearly during the April 1991 dispute when the company initially wanted the strike — basically over a rejected JIC recommendation — to go to the Labour Court which covered disputes in the wider industrial sectors. The major management criticism is borne out by the comment of a senior executive who said that "so long as everything is kept in between these walls its recommendations are always going to have regard to what is happening in here and not outside". The union view is that during the 1980s that the best chance you had at the council was of a "fifty per cent deal". In other words, they felt they were literally forced to refer issues and cases to the council because of management's refusal to negotiate under the "no give policy". Management strategy for dealing with many of the claims that came before them was outlined by an executive with broad experience of claims in distribution:

> The way we play the game is to draw out the negotiations as long as possible so that by the time you reach agreement you will pay out a lot less than if you had reached agreement within a month or so. This has been a conscious decision and we play the procedures so that when a settlement is reached you might not pay as much though you might pay. But you might pay in other ways in terms of morale.

In terms of the impact of the high usage of the Joint Industrial Council on formal and informal relations at shop floor and station floor level, one senior figure on the distribution side says that

right through the 1980s the system had centralised from an earlier period when more issues were dealt with locally. The result, in
his view, was that relationships at local level were reduced in
terms of stature and importance through that process. This erosion of personal relations at local level between middle managers
and staff was in the view of many responsible for the failure of
management intelligence to pick up that the April 1991 strike was
coming. But it had a deeper impact in terms of the perception of
the centralised personnel department and its role as one person
noted:

> Staff no longer saw that solutions and their relationships were
> really within the plant. You had a system of by-pass, which in-
> creasingly became the focus of what was going on. People were
> going up to Dublin, using the Industrial Council more and more
> to a point where what was happening was the takeover of the
> whole personnel management function by the centralised func-
> tion.

One senior union figure with members in all the major categories
said that the majority of big issues went to the Council; the company in accepting everything gave people the impression that they
had nothing to lose. This had put the Council itself in an invidious
position. While he personally believed that the management policy
of accepting every Council recommendation was unusual, the
Council had provided a great internal stability in ESB industrial
relations.

A trade unionist from outside the ESB with an intimate knowledge of the workings of the Board describes the industrial relations climate operating in the company up to recently as reminis-
cent of the 1970s in terms of the adherence to formal procedures,
every change having a price and all major issues being sucked into
the industrial relations system. While the Labour Court had been
looked upon in this light outside the ESB in the 1970s, this was no
longer the situation. The situation had changed dramatically now,
not alone in the private sector but in the public sector with issues
being dealt with locally or directly across the table.

The 1988 ESBOA Dispute Over Numbers

A dispute with the ESB Officers Association (ESBOA) in November 1988 saw management adopting one of its hardest and most
public stances in the face of action by clerical staff over a plan to
reduce numbers. The dispute is significant, not alone for manage-

ment seeking to define its right to introduce change unilaterally,
but for the way it attempted to use the opportunity presented by
the row to deal with long-standing problems with the union involved. After 400 staff had been withdrawn from the computer
centre, head office departments, Distribution regions and four
power stations, the Chief Executive told the Board that it was the
"unanimous view of ESB management that the proper management of the business through the implementation of change was
being obstructed by the ESBOA". The minimum that was required
from the union was that the strike be called off, the threat of two
further strikes be withdrawn and that there be acceptance by
ESBOA of "certain fundamental management rights to implement
change", the Board was told. The Chief Executive put forward a
series of proposals to the union during the dispute and warned
that if the ESBOA did not accept these it was:

> Time to have an independent public inquiry so that the cus-
> tomers got an unbiased view of the whole situation in the ESB.
> My colleagues and I unanimously want a public inquiry now if
> our final proposals are rejected.

The Board's position was that they had made all reasonable concessions and would not go into negotiations with the ESBOA until
the strike was over and then only on the terms of the management
memorandum. From the management perspective the strike —
over the planned reductions in numbers, part of the 1984 Miller
Barry plan — was "totally unjustified" because it was based on the
presumption that industrial action was necessary to protect jobs.
Cast-iron guarantees over security had been given to every member of staff and the union had even failed to operate agreed procedures. If the union rejected the management's proposals, the
unanimous management view was that "the community must face
up to such blackmail if it arises". Power supplies had not been
threatened but this was to be the next part of the union's plan.

During the dispute the Chief Executive took out advertise-
ments in the public press in the form of a letter to customers
where he talked of the ESBOA seeking a "veto on every change
planned" and he also questioned the nature of the "slim" yes vote
on which the union had launched the dispute. The ESB made
special arrangements for the payment of non-ESBOA staff despite
the pay section being hit and issued special circulars to ESBOA
members returning to work on a rotating basis, asking them to
give a written guarantee to work normally.

The ESB declined to allow the case go forward to the Joint Industrial Council because the ESBOA "had a history of rejecting JIC recommendations" and because they had a threat of strike in two further cases where JIC recommendations had been rejected. The Board would only allow a referral of the case to the Joint Industrial Council if there was an agreement in advance to accept its recommendation. After a Labour Court investigation, at the request of the ICTU, and an interim recommendation the ESBOA agreed to call off its dispute and the ESB provided the union with a copy of its activity review giving a breakdown of staffing in each location.

The nub of the union's case was that it had a right to negotiate fully on job numbers and change, not just on the impact or effect of management decisions on reductions in staffing. Following a full investigation, the Labour Court in a comprehensive recommendation found that the dispute could have been avoided if "the ESB had agreed to negotiate on numbers or if the ESBOA had agreed to examine and negotiate on numbers at local level only" (LCR, 12165: 8). The ESBOA had misunderstood the nature of the activity review, which had not dealt with numbers but was nothing more than a compilation of results from different locations. In a judgement on the "Framework for Relationships between the ESBOA and ESB" document, issued by the Board but rejected by the union during the dispute, the Court found that the ESBOA "must be allowed to retain the right to take industrial action in defence of its members' basic and fundamental interests". It found that the ESB proposals dated 14 November:

> Do not clearly preserve that right and the Court does not consider them reasonable and does not therefore recommend these proposals as a long term solution to the difficulties in the relationships between the parties (LCR, 12165: 12).

Overall the Court said that it was an essential part of the recommendation that the management of the ESB should agree to make greater use of the scope for consultation on appropriate issues (LCR, 12165: 13). However the recommendation was to be nothing more than a "fix" for the dispute and did not lead to any new consultative process or any formal review of the management's IR policy. The thinking behind the management approach to the ESBOA action was summed up by one senior executive who said that by the late 1980s many senior executives believed that the company had been "too soft on them":

The ESBOA were running with too many cases and we always seemed to be conceding to them and that was a very strong view throughout the management. There was a feeling that the ESBOA could close down the place and that if necessary they should be made aware that the place could be run without them. That is an underlying view that no group on their own should ever feel that they can shut the country down. It makes them very powerful and this is what happens with particular groups. The attitude in the 80s was that we had to face up to these problems and this is what happened in the OA. There was a strong united front. The ESBOA were getting far too powerful.

Moneypoint's 1989 Unofficial Action

An unofficial dispute in the giant Moneypoint station, whose three units provide one third of national power demand, resulted in a major risk to supplies in September 1989. The row centred on a demand by general workers at the plant for more overtime to work with craftsmen, mainly electricians. It resulted in the complete shutting down of the station, the largest in the country. The management regarded the issue in dispute as very basic: a question of "order versus chaos in employee relations". The workers involved had totally ignored industrial relations procedures and had not raised the problem locally with management before placing pickets. An informal solution was agreed on a Thursday evening but dishonoured the following morning.

The management saw the dispute in terms of defending the industrial relations procedures which had been freely negotiated. About half of the station's 350 staff stayed out in support of the general workers. The dispute, eventually sorted out by national union officials who obtained a return to work followed by later discussions, was linked to the tradition of high overtime among general workers during the construction on the site. Some of these general workers had gone on to work for the ESB and were accustomed to peaks of high overtime earnings, shift allowances and features like completion bonuses (*Business and Finance*, 28 September 1989). In late 1991 Moneypoint station, after a series of unofficial actions, was selected by the Chief Executive for a special change initiative, which is examined in detail in Chapter Eight in the wider context of the emergence of Human Resource Management.

Conclusion

The Liberal Pluralist model for the conduct of industrial relations assumed dominance in the ESB in the early 1970s, an era of growth, lack of sensitivity on prices and stable market conditions with benign Government support. The system functioned well but at a cost; the most minor changes created bargaining opportunities and "money washed away issues" through management concessions. Reform, as Batstone (1988) noted, did not lead to a reduction in bargaining but increased it considerably. Developments from 1983 in the Board highlighted the weaknesses of its highly internalised system of bargaining, and crystallised a growing management disillusionment with the process, particularly the Joint Industrial Council. Management's "no give policy" and the referral of all major issues to the Council suggests that real bargaining largely ceased. Pluralist thinking, on the other hand, suggested that every problem would produce its own compromise. Developments within ESB challenge conventional theory on this point. The problems encountered in securing change through the conventional bargaining channels ultimately produced a response in the side of the company facing the greatest external challenge — generation. Before considering the strike itself and the crisis in bargaining relations it exposed in Chapter Six, the introduction of this alternative management strategy is considered next in Chapter Five.

Chapter Five

EUROPEAN DEREGULATION AND THE EMERGENCE OF HUMAN RESOURCE MANAGEMENT

Introduction

Many of the challenges posed to the pluralist bargaining orthodoxy of semi-state firms in recent years have their origin outside the companies themselves and in emerging European deregulation and Government demands to meet more clearly defined commercial criteria. The threats posed by these external forces to the traditional industrial relations agenda have taken many different forms: in demands for numerical flexibility, the contracting out of non-essential tasks and greater worker flexibility and multi-skilling. Many of these initiatives are associated with a human resource management approach to employee relations, which is gaining an increasing foothold in management strategies and emphasizes shared goals between shopfloor and management, trust and the need for ongoing change. In some firms this new approach is being operated in parallel with traditional bargaining mechanisms, in others it has supplanted them. The roots of the human resource management initiative in the ESB were both internal and external, and linked to difficulties in the conventional bargaining agenda exposed by the 1991 strike as well as impending de-regulation.

The beginnings and rise of human resource management (HRM) thinking in the ESB can be traced to the major difficulties encountered by management in securing change in the late 1980s. This alternative management approach originated largely outside the Personnel Directorate, which had traditionally carried responsibility for employee relations and operated to pluralist principles. While Personnel had debated the usefulness of an alternative strategy in a company-wide context, HRM was to be given its most concrete expression on the side of the business which faced the greatest threat from dawning European competition and de-regulation and which confronted the greatest industrial relations problems: the Directorate responsible for generation. The back-drop to the new initiative on the generation side of the business was the dawning realisation that the surplus capacity which had allowed the company to live with certain restrictive work practices in power stations since 1981 was being progressively eroded, as demand gradually increased.

At a European level, the demand for transparency in costs through the separation of generation from distribution, facilitating access by new independent entrants to the business, was also cited as a reason for trying an alternative approach. European Commission proposals were to have major structural implications for the ESB, particularly the later move to divide the company into five business units and the reduction of the size of head office from over 1,000 to around 100 staff. Indeed, as we shall see later, the plan to implement the Commission's proposals in the company, drawn up by McKinsey consultants, was itself heavily imbued with HRM thinking. As well as seeking greater commitment and teamworking, the linkage of personal performance goals and rewards to business goals was heavily stressed by McKinsey in the new, more commercially driven environment (McKinsey, 1992: Exhibit 24).

Management in generation felt it could not sustain the expensive work practices restrictions that had existed in stations, particularly in relation to the hiring of outside contractors to shorten maintenance cycles, because the surplus plant would no longer exist. Availability of plant, particularly the larger units, is regarded by the company as the key to greater efficiency in production and to price effectiveness. Moreover, plant performance has a major impact on overall company performance: a one per cent rise in output in Moneypoint Power Station results in an annual saving in operating costs of £1.2 million. Across the system a similar improvement could result in capital avoidance of around £30 million over 10 years. In these circumstances the company believed it could not justify investment in new plant as the existing stations were not operating to full capacity.

Having tried to introduce change through the standard industrial relations agenda within the ESB without success, the management on the generation side decided to develop and pursue their own policy which they felt was more appropriate to their business and the unique conditions within which it operated. Power station managers were to be the major instigators of change and were given responsibility for implementing the new approach on the ground. A number of concrete measures were put in place at station level aimed at opening up communications and better flows of information. One major barrier was a 1981 agreement with fitters which imposed tight limits on what could be done by outside contractors. Overtime hours equivalent to the hours worked by the contractors were guaranteed, which in itself represented a huge additional pay cost and took, in many cases, years to work off. An initiative from generation management to surmount the obstacle posed by this deal, in the form of an offer of a £10,000 lump sum and a five per cent rise, was a significant contributory factor to the April 1991 electricians' dispute. That offer was opposed by the Director of Personnel at the highest level. It represents a clash arising from the "dualist" strategy which took hold in the generation business from the late 1980s. Before considering the evolution of HRM in the Board overall in detail, and in its largest station, this chapter seeks to outline the backdrop to the greater competitive pressure faced by the ESB in generation.

Apart from the more domestic factors, the impetus for change and a re-assessment of structures in the ESB came from abroad, and particularly from developments at European level. These were aimed at opening up the electricity supply industry to new independent operators, and were based on the view that in the electricity sector, the prevailing relationships between production, transmission, distribution and supply do not allow more than limited competition.

The European Commission's Proposals

Over 20 years had elapsed since the adoption of the Treaty of Rome before the Commission addressed directives or decisions of member states under Article 90 (3). The Transparency Directive in 1980 obliged states to clarify their financial relationship with public undertakings, and any funds provided would have to be justified under state aid rules. Water, energy, postal, telecommunications and transport sectors were excluded from the scope of the directive until it was amended in 1985.

In 1988 in a working document, "The Internal Market" (May 1988), the Commission stressed its determination to apply the competition rules more strictly than in the past in order to achieve greater integration in the energy market.

In 1990 in the first phase of the liberalisation of the electricity sector, the Council adopted directives facilitating the transit of electricity (Council Directive 90/547/EEC of 29 October 1990) and

improving the transparency of gas and electricity prices for industrial customers. The aim of the Transit Directive, which was formally implemented in Ireland by the European Communities
(Transit of Electricity) Regulations 1991, was to permit a generating company in Germany to sell power to a customer in Spain. But
the lack of an interconnector into the Irish system means that this
provision had no practical effect here at the moment.

The second phase of liberalisation was initiated by the issue of
a draft directive in January 1992, obliging member states to take
positive action by adopting measures to ensure that vertically integrated utilities must "unbundle" — that is, separate the management and accounting of the production, transmission and distribution activities. This provision is regarded as an essential element to ensure transparency of operations but ownership structures will not be affected. The proposals envisaged a limited role
for intervention by member states. One area for domestic influence was the possibility of ordering the priority utilisation of indigenous resources of electricity generation for up to 20 per cent of
overall needs. This provision is expected to apply to the utilisation
of peat in ESB electricity generation, which sustains about 800
jobs in the Midlands. This opt-out for indigenous fuels is to be reduced to 15 per cent of needs after the year 2000.

The final proposal in this second stage allowed for the introduction of third party access (TPA) to certain large energy consumers whose consumption exceeded a certain threshold and to
distribution companies under certain conditions. This final branch
of the Commission's proposal is the most controversial within the
industry, effectively permitting an external generator to have access to the national network in order to reach its customer.

The McKinsey report, *Reshaping ESB to Meet the Challenges of
the 1990s*, published in July 1992, was the ESB's response to the
Government review of the restructuring options for the Irish electricity industry in the light of EC de-regulatory developments. The
Minister for Energy of the day, Robert Molloy, had hired another
firm of consultants, Coopers and Lybrand, to look at the future
shape of the Board. The view in both the company and the wider
political arena was that he favoured a break up of the Board into
two separate companies. The Minister later aired this view publicly saying "there would be considerable benefit for consumers if
the generation activities of ESB were seperated from their transmission and distribution functions" (*Irish Independent* and *Irish
Times*, 8 February 1992). He also believed that there was scope for

competition in the generation business and that there was no need for a monopoly. The McKinsey report was the ESB's contribution to the Minister's review process. It was also, it will be argued in Chapter Six, part of a damage limitation exercise by management in the immediate post strike climate. Overall, the roots of the McKinsey proposals for the future shape of the ESB — with its emphasis on profit centres, decentralizing decision-making and a smaller head office — are to be found in "Connecting with the Future — ESB Strategies for the 1990s" published in March 1990.

Separate Companies and Cultures

Underlying the move to the commitment model was a tacit acknowledgement that the generation side of the ESB was in effect "a company within a company" with its own culture and ethos, quite separate from the more visible distribution business, which was closer to the customer, less isolated and produced less intractable IR problems. Generating stations are highly institutionalised operations working to clearly defined rule books with clear distinctions existing between the various categories of staff who work in them. As one executive put it:

> Power plants are closed societies compared to the very different, extroverted and widely distributed population in customer services.

Generation management were arriving at the conclusion that treating the company as one unit for the purposes of implementing broad industrial relations or personnel strategy might no longer hold. The focus of the IR system had been in Dublin but executives now felt that problems should be dealt with locally by management and unions. Comparing units like Moneypoint and Poolbeg was impossible, and the answer to local difficulties had to be found within the local context. The view from generation was that the centralised personnel function was heavily loaded into traditional industrial relations thinking with an overall company perspective. This key role in the industrial relations maze had hampered the development of strategic thinking and the creation of fresh solutions. In essence, the view was that because of the different business parameters, distribution did not call for the same degree of change. As power generation was a capital intensive business there was a need for this directorate to create its own HRM strategy.

Eventually, in late 1990, the New Generation Programme, which pin-pointed the achievement of availability targets from power stations as the key strategic issue facing generation management in the 1990s, was published. A target of 82 per cent availability was set for thermal plant and 90 per cent for hydro plant through the reduction of forced and scheduled outages. In the larger units scheduled outages were expected not to exceed six weeks.

It became apparent to management on the generating side in the late 1980s that to try and achieve the standards of performance necessary to defer investment in new plant, they could not rely solely on achieving progress through industrial relations. They regarded it as too expensive and too slow. Instead, a parallel approach to industrial relations was initiated, aimed at bringing about a change in culture. As one executive associated with the new approach explained:

> We saw that the generation business, the power stations, had a particular culture and that this culture would have to be managed and changed if we were to achieve performance improvement. Hence the twin track approach.

The 1989 Special Working Group

A Special Working group (initially known as the Development Group) was set up in 1989 with the aim of improving plant availability under the Assistant Chief Operations Officer. The ambition was to achieve a level of improvement in the performance of the workforce that had been achieved in the other systems. The emphasis was to be on improving plant availability. When demand growth exhausted the surplus plant margin, all necessary plant maintenance would have to be carried out within the natural maintenance opportunity, if the provision of new plant was to be avoided. Priority was to be given to the creation of a sound employee relations climate which would have to be developed if the high standard of performance sought was to be achieved. And progress was to be made on the promotion of greater flexibility and the elimination of category barriers. "Multi-skilling" within power stations was to be researched and definite proposals brought foward on appropriate manning guidelines. Transcending all of these changes was what the document called "an absolute requirement for the managerial environment to change". The new focus on power stations as business units was to be sharpened, and linked by a "transfer of ownership" of corporate policy, managerial discretion and the devolution of authority.

In essence, without corrective action the company would not be able to meet output targets, and would have to carry increased plant margins bringing foward the need for new plant and consequent major capital expenditure. Each extra 50 megawatts of plant would involve a capital cost of between £13 million and £43 million depending on the type of plant purchased. There was some validity in the perception, the report found, that the Board had already paid for some productivity elements in previous agreements which they had not yet achieved.

To give practical expression to the strategy outlined by the Special Working Group, a separate Working Party was established consisting of four station managers and this produced a report in January 1991 entitled "Management of Change in Power Stations". The report's analysis concluded that:

> In the power stations there is a hierarchical culture with an all pervasive industrial relations environment and mutual lack of trust in official/management staff relations. Also the dominance of overtime in the reward system is at odds with the station objective of minimum plant outage time (Management of Change in Power Stations, 1991: 2).

Deficiencies in management skills were identified; all levels of management had been appointed without training in human resource management and presentation skills. Team effort in stations was being weakened by category allegiances among staff, and management were not being trusted when conveying corporate information. Generation management sought to ground their HRM strategy through station managers.

Management of Change in Power Stations

The New Generation Programme, which was part of generation's overall HRM initiative, gave rise to the introduction of the Station Performance Incentive (SPI), a scheme under which additional annual payments were made to staff in particular stations for improvements in output and a reduction in the number of forced outages — the number of unplanned non-generation days. Payments of up to six per cent of basic pay were available on meeting strict criteria. A further off-shoot of the New Generation Programme — an offer to fitters to allow more widespread use of outside contractors to shorten maintenance cycles in stations — was to present a

major problem for the Personnel Department, cutting as it did
across their direct negotiating field. The major fear from the personnel standpoint was that a proposed offer of five per cent and
£10,000 for fitters would have had huge knock on implications for
other groups. Firm opposition to the move was expressed and the
issue was taken up with the Chief Executive. The emergence on
the negotiating table informally of the offer to fitters was one of
the influences behind the 1991 dispute. But generation took a different view:

> Our thinking was that unlocking the 1981 deal was the key to
> change and the introduction of HRM initiatives. We tried to
> move foward on both fronts at the same time. In retrospect it
> was probably naive, but we did think we had the possibility of
> cutting a deal with the fitters.

Thus the decade of the 1980s, which had opened with a reaffirma-
tion of pluralist principles through a new comprehensive agreement for the entire company, ended with the beginnings of an alternative management strategy being developed for the half of the
business that presented the most intractable difficulties. Both the
generation and personnel functions shared the growing disillusionment with the existing system. But it was the erosion of spare
capacity and the failure of the conventional bargaining agenda to
yield progress on greater plant utilisation that provided the
opening. However, the perspectives from the personnel management and generation management side of how to handle the
problem were quite different.

The Personnel Perspective

From the point-of-view of the Personnel Department there was
always a perceived reluctance on the part of generation to appoint
people with experience on the distribution side to management
positions as they became vacant. They were seen as people who,
because of their engineering bias, perceived problems in more
complex terms than the situation often required. This often involved setting up Task Forces, which from an outside perspective
achieved little. In short, they saw the most complex solution to
every problem and could not see simple ones. One executive said
that he recognised that generation had been trying to change the
culture; but he was not certain that they "knew what culture they
wanted".

The Director of Personnel had produced a document in 1988 which supported a strategic position not dissimilar to the New Generation Programme, albeit stated in slightly different terms. His central approach can be summarised as building a continuously adaptable organisation which is market driven, utilizes high technology and is innovation based; the creation of a flatter and less hierarchical structure; achieving a highly flexible workforce; and a pay structure which is motivational and geared towards results and rewards effort. The HRM model being considered by personnel was in many ways a purer form of HRM than what was being pursued by generation, based as it was on company wide approach and the interlinking of all the key variables being driven company wide.

Management Strategy in Context: 1970-91

The burst of reform in ESB industrial relations in the late 1960s, epitomised by the setting up of the Joint Industrial Council and the first comprehensive agreement, were all inspired by the Fogarty Report published in 1969 which was in effect an Irish Donovan. The Fogarty report itself was a response to an internal crisis within the Board which expressed itself in the frequency of disputes. But while accepting the broad thrust of the Committee's conclusions and the new agenda it set for the conduct of industrial relations, the unions forced the Government's hand and successfully fought a proposal in the interim report that in future rows should go to the Labour Court. Thus at a stroke they won a measure which guaranteed the "internalisation" of company IR problems and avoided exposure of the company's claims in a forum used by the rest of industry.

The positive and benign mood which permeated management/union relations in the company for the first half of the 1970s sprang in part from the zeal with which Fogarty was being implemented by both sides, as well as from the novelty of bedding in the range of new procedures. But the price of a positive and progressive industrial relations environment appeared to be overmaning, when by 1975 the oil crisis forced the management into announcing 1500 job cuts. There were financial resources available to fund a variety of new deals, as the price of developing new relationships.

The greater formalisation of industrial relations system led to more claims being lodged through procedures. This is consistent with Batstone's finding from the UK that reform did not lead to a

reduction in shop floor bargaining but instead resulted in a rise in
activity (Batstone, 1988: 134). Towards the end of the decade
management complained of the unions rejecting or questioning
every Joint Industrial Council recommendation which they had
accepted. Minor changes were being turned into bargaining opportunities and expectations took no account of the broader picture in
the wider economy. This was expressed in the form of
"opportunism in claim derivation, apparent in the commodifica-
tion of social values or the tendency to put price tags on all
changes in the job" (Roche, 1987: 395). This in turn would appear
to confirm the view that the existence of union and management
superstructures on either side tended to encourage each other's
growth (Batstone 1988:64). However, by 1980, the Board reviewed
its personnel policy in the light of more difficult market conditions. The process of disillusionment had begun. As one figure
close to policy development at the time put it:

> By the end of the 1970s management had implemented every-
> thing that Fogarty had wanted but they were not getting the
> reciprocation. And when the crises of the early 1980s arose the
> view from on top was that change was going to be driven by as-
> sertive management without much reference to the unions.

The decline in industrial relations activity in the early 1980s was
partly attributable to the introduction of a comprehensive agreement, based on the brighter emerging growth prospects. This high
point of pluralism, during which "money washed away issues",
was later superseded by a regime of restructuring, based on the
need to reduce costs. The period from the late 1970s up to the ex-
piry of the deal in 1984 probably demonstrates in Metcalf's phrase
that "formalisation meant management concessions rather than
being a vehicle to greater co-operation and higher productivity"
(Metcalf, 1989: 8). The external climatic change that shook the
system, just when Joint Industrial Council pay claims reached
their 400 peak per annum, emerged in the form of a drop in demand and public criticism of pricing policy. This triggered a management review of structures which cast a spotlight on the rigidities of the IR system and led to an open questioning by management. The internal "toughening up" of management's position was
mirrored by outside developments, and a greater questioning of
the role of the State sector in the political system and in particular
of State monopolies.

The rise of human resource management techniques is directly attributable to the competitive threat from changes in the structure of the European electricity generation as it emerged in the late 1980s and the blockage on the conventional bargaining agenda. The new thinking developed on the side of the business which was most exposed to external changes and competition, and in particular to the fall-out from European developments in deregulation. But the trigger that led to an alternative personnel strategy being sought, was the erosion of the surplus generation capacity through rising demand. Because electricity generation is more capital than labour intensive, its planning time frame for new capacity forced it into adopting a more strategic approach to the management of its business. Distribution, by definition a "downstream" activity from generation, could operate with a more passive management style. It sold a single product delivered across a single transmission system by a staff that lived close by the customer, and ultimately was less powerful. Culturally and environmentally it was very different to the more intense atmosphere of generation.

Thus the introduction of HRM into the ESB fits into the textbook case of transformative industrial relations, where external market changes forced a reappraisal of fundamental approach towards employee relations. Developments in the ESB meet Walton's argument regarding increased competitive pressure as a force in moving firms towards the commitment model. The ESB was changing from a single product monopolistic bureaucracy to a company where its key commercial customers, under deregulation, could openly negotiate on price with outside competitors.

The hegemony of pluralism, on the other hand, is best seen in the context of a stable and largely unchanging market with little price sensitivity, allied to a stable technological environment where change can be predicted and be prepared for over time. In the case of the ESB, its dominance can be explained by its role in a centralised structure for collective bargaining and firm union, and in some cases management resistance to change. There is also an age factor attaching to its longevity: an entire generation of ESB managers and union officials of similar age grew up with the machinery of traditional bargaining created in 1970. Staff expectations and management's aspirations for change were mediated through the conventional wisdom that surrounded it. And when a crisis struck, both sides resorted to the traditional levers. The timing of the 1991 strike, and the range of other unfinished business it exposed, meant that the traditional methods of solving disputes in the ESB proved to be totally deficient in creating a resolution. This weakness in the system was further exacerbated by the huge public outcry the strike produced.

The operation of HRM policies in the ESB, albeit on the side of the business facing the most dramatic change alongside traditional collective bargaining, is a clear example of the sort of "dualism" outlined by John Storey (1992: 258) and Terry Cradden (1992: 43). The case of the ESB, with traditional IR policy being run from personnel, and HRM initially from generation, would appear to be a clear example of the "dual dealing" Storey encountered in British research.

The breakout of the strike, just as an alternative HRM approach was being developed and bedded down in power stations, meant that management at the most senior level had an alternative strategy to resort to for the whole company in their hour of crisis. The handling of the dispute by personnel, and the unprecedented public and political response to the severity of the power cuts, ultimately tipped the balance away from up to then traditional method of resolving disputes.

Conclusion

The alteration of management strategy within generation ultimately led to a strategic change in the policy for managing staff within the Board as a whole. Having outlined the internal pressures and external forces forging change on the side of the business facing the greatest competitive threat, the next chapter seeks to outline the catalyst for the switch to an overall HRM policy within the Board as a whole; the 1991 strike itself. We will return to the issue of the introduction of HRM later, when the proposals outlined by the Cassells Review of Relationships Report and McKinsey Consultants, and the structures within which the new policy was introduced, are considered in Chapter Seven. The forces shaping its implementation at the level of the individual station will be considered in the final empirical chapter, Chapter Eight.

Chapter Six

MANAGEMENT RE-ALIGNMENT AND THE 1991 DISPUTE

Introduction

Having assessed the major external forces for change in the ESB in Chapter Five in terms of de-regulation and increased competition, which have also impacted on other semi-states recently, notably TEAM and Irish Steel, the role of a major strike is considered next. Disputes as major triggers for change and shifts in management strategy have received relatively little attention in the literature, but, as we saw in Chapter One, have played some part in recent Irish industrial relations experience. When the full history of TEAM Aer Lingus is written, the role of the summer 1994 dispute in altering management's approach will be significant. The 1991 ESB strike was no less momentous and is seen in retrospect as the catalyst which led to the Government review of the entire electricity industry in Ireland and of the Board's cost structure. The fall-out from these two initiatives are now being grappled with. It has led to a major review of relationships and of the traditional pluralist model for conducting management/union relations.

The 1991 electricians' strike stands out as a watershed dispute in the recent industrial relations history of the ESB in terms of its impact and consequences. The four day action, which turned into a public relations disaster for the company, has been a major factor in the transformation of industrial relations in the Board in the three years since it occurred. Failure to predict its emergence undermined the credibility and authority of the personnel function, putting the dominance of traditional industrial relations approaches seriously at risk. The strike momentum crystallised a growing disillusionment with the norms and operation of the existing pluralist IR system, and resulted in a review of relations which backed fundamental change. While leaving the basic structures intact, this report supported an essentially unitarist HRM approach opening up new channels of communication, trust and participation.

Union acceptance of its findings paved the way for acceptance in principle of a plan to split the ESB into five divisions, each with its own management and personnel structure. Without the dispute and the public and political reaction it unleashed, the unions would not have accepted the decision to split the company into divisions. Thus, it can be argued that the shock and crisis to the system the 1991 dispute represented generated a major shift in approach to the management of people and left lasting consequences. Overall, the strike outcome put supporters of an alternative HRM approach in the ascendant, and seriously undermined any residual belief that traditional IR practices alone would deliver the changes required for the foreseeable future. In addition to forcing a permanent change in personnel strategy, the ferocity of the public outcry against the strike resulted in the partial abandonment of one of the core principles contained in the 1969 Fogarty Report on the ESB — namely, that it should be willing to accept disruption to supplies as an alternative to conceding "unjust" demands.

In particular, it brought to the surface a growing disenchantment among senior personnel executives, which had been present since the early 1980s, about the difficulty of winning change and reforming a highly structured system. This in part led to management's highly stressed response to the 1988 dispute with the ESBOA on numbers, and its toughest expression of the "no give policy" which had operated since 1983. The timing of the 1991 dispute, and management's failure to detect that it was coming, undermined confidence in the joint rule making procedures which had served the Board since 1970, and which were being operated in less that total good faith from 1980 on. This chapter attempts to outline the major development of the 1991 dispute and its impact on the pluralist management strategy which has held sway since 1970 and the shock to the system it represented.

The ESB strike of April 1991, which began as a row over the measurement and payment for past productivity, ended up as a major test of not only company management but of the Board's own industrial relations machinery and procedures, and more specifically of national pay policy and the PESP. Billed by management as "a strike that was never going to happen", its conduct, settlement and aftermath were to have a lasting impact both inside and outside the Board. Internally, it led to a Joint Review of Industrial Relations and a reassessment by management of the dominance of traditional IR culture and practises, while externally it provided an impetus to the formulation of national Codes of Practice for essential services. At a Government or regulatory level it led to a fresh examination of the ESB's structure, its multi-layered bargaining procedure and its role as a monopoly provider of electricity since 1927. The rapid escalation of the week long dispute, its public handling by the union and management and its settlement through ministerial and political intervention, all suggest it had some unique characteristics. Many of these are only to be found in the highly politically charged atmosphere of Irish public sector pay bargaining.

Immediate Background

The Electrical Trade Union (ETU), which later became the Technical Engineering and Electrical Union (TEEU), has slightly over 22,000 members, 1,579 of them in the ESB. It had not been involved in launching strike action in the Board since 1960. About two-thirds of its membership in the ESB are electricians, but only around 150 were employed in power generation with the remainder working in distribution. Also involved were the then three month old Labour Relations Commission, the Board's own dispute settling machinery, the Joint Industrial Council (JIC), and latterly the Irish Congress of Trades Unions, of which the TEEU was an affiliate member. The TEEU itself was regarded as a particularly hard union to deal with by ESB management, which believed it suffered from "tunnel vision" and was "mesmerised" by the protection of the craft of electricians and saw any change as an infringement of traditional duties.

The issue at the centre of the April 1991 dispute was a five per cent pay claim sought by the TEEU in compensation for changes introduced by management in the preceding four years. It was the formal rejection of this claim by the Joint Industrial Council that was to spark the strike. Under a 1986 agreement between the TEEU and the Board, a six per cent rise over and above other increases was introduced for electricians. Under this agreement, either party could seek a review within two years and the TEEU exercised this option in 1988. The union maintained that the changes brought in over the intervening years had affected its members, and further pay rises were sought to ensure their continued co-operation. This had resulted in a 25 per cent reduction in staffing levels and 20 per cent increase in consumption according to the union. The TEEU had also sought a review of pay structures to keep them ahead of other less specialised groups such as drivers and linesmen.

Talks continued for over two years, with management arguing that the changes had not affected the electricians as much as had been claimed. Fear of knock-ons for other grades was one of the management's grounds for opposing the claim. Moreover, the ESB was engaged in talks with other groups who had real productivity to sell, and could not be seen to entertain a claim for past productivity while negotiating future change with more vital groupings. After direct talks failed the matter was referred to the Board's Joint Industrial Council which recommended a small rise for the electricians. The Council, which is comprised of management and union representatives, stated that the company should award one point on the payment scale to the TEEU, worth about £300, with those at the top of the scale getting £650. The key final paragraph of the determination of the Joint Industrial Council in case 2233(b) said that the terms of the overall recommendation could be reviewed by request of either party two years from the date of acceptance. But the "out" that this provision offered was never really explored.

Strike Notice is Served

The company accepted the JIC recommendation as it generally accepted other awards from the Council, but the TEEU in a ballot rejected it, regarding the sum as derisory and not meeting their key demand for an ongoing payment. They invoked the 30 day "cooling off period" allowed for in internal ESB procedures. Before the mandatory period was over, the TEEU wrote to the management notifying them of their intention to take action within two weeks. But the management, believing that the TEEU would not garner any great support, and mindful of previous occasions when other workers had not passed pickets for the first 48 hours, was still assuring the public on Sunday, 20 April that there would be no power cuts. The following 24 hours were to demonstrate how wrong they were.

Pinpointing the reasons for management's failure to grasp the gravity of the strike threat is more difficult. Decentralisation of the personnel function and failure to understand the impact that the non-completion of category talks and other negotiations with the unions were having in terms of feeling on the ground was also a factor in the management miscalculation. Complacency towards the danger posed by the TEEU strike notice was another factor.

One outside observer with subsequent experience of developments pointed to what he regarded as an important element of the problem:

> Part of it was that managers were judged by their performance and in terms of how well they were resolving the difficulties. However no one would be reporting back to head office on problems that could not be resolved therefore the two levels were out of sync in a sense.

A breakdown in the upward flow of information through the management system was believed by many to be the root of the problem. A senior figure on the union side believed that the previous major dispute in 1987 provided certain insights which were not fully acted on:

> Arrogance was the reason they did not know the dispute was coming. There were continually being told but they kept up the "kick them" approach. They tried to take away the idea that people worked in secure employment and hounded good guys out. After 35 years a sullen resentment began to build up that you could not solve problems. The first indication they got that things were wrong was in 1987 but people went out the next day and forgot the lessons.

Nevertheless once the dispute started, staff backed their more powerful colleagues in the power stations. The failure of one group, supervisors, to pass the word of the impending difficulty up the management chain was particularly evident in retrospect to many senior executives. Many trade union leaders and not a few managers have highlighted the failure to develop informal personal relationships as a key element in the company's lack of intelligence about what was happening on the ground in the run up to the 1991 action. Management's perception of the rigidity of the industrial relations system and their decision to operate the "no give policy" in response may have played a part in this attitude. Both these factors appear to have played a part in the "freezing up" of the system of industrial relations in the Board in the late 1980s, in which personnel management felt entrapped in a system they had little faith in but had no option but to work with. Ultimately this mood, and the pressure of standard day-to-day fire-fighting duties of industrial relations, may have left personnel executives with little time to think of alternatives. One internal review in the wake of the dispute, which influenced the Cassells Report, found that:

Middle and front line managers are afraid to bring bad news to their superiors. This is one of the reasons they underestimated the support for the TEEU strike.

However, among the specific factors which influenced the strike decision was the earlier offer to fitters of a £10,000 lump sum and a five per cent pay rise and the perceived threat to the Joint Industrial Council process from a management decision in 1990, later reversed, not to allow a 20 per cent pay claim by clerical staff, be considered by the Council.

The Joint Industrial Council's (JIC) Role

At one level the management was operating to the central tenet of the Fogarty report by standing up to the claim, and defending the internal dispute settling machinery — the JIC. In reality, however management were becoming increasingly disillusioned with the existing JIC framework. It had become the major focus of the disenchantment felt by many industrial relations managers, principally because of the "no risk" element attached to cases brought before the Council. In the late 1980s senior personnel executives drew up detailed submissions making a case for reform of the Joint Industrial Council, and outlined reasons why management should demonstrate its independence by rejecting a recommendation. The deficiencies of the JIC process became something of a fixation within the personnel function and among those who were seeking reform. It may have hampered more strategic thinking of the type that was to later emerge from outside the personnel domain.

This impatience with the existing machinery was to become obvious in the 1991 strike in a very stark fashion. The third day of the action, Wednesday, 24 April, saw a public clash between the ESB's Director of Personnel and the Chief Executive of the Labour Relations Commission about the future direction of the peace process. By 11.00 am, after an all night session, the Personnel Director said that he believed that the talks were failing in the Commission forum and he wanted the row referred to the Labour Court. The Commission's Chief Executive appealed to both sides to adopt a lower profile in the dispute and to avoid negotiation over the airwaves. The ESB, having first wanted the row to go back into the Board's own machinery, the Joint Industrial Council, now wanted it to go to the Labour Court. A proposal put privately by the ESB in the early hours of the morning was never received by the union. The company in turn felt that the union had rejected its overture and then went public calling for a referral to the Court. As the talks broke up around 2.30 am on 25 April, it emerged that the TEEU wanted to bring their case back to the JIC, but management were opposed to this move. This major change of approach by management within days of the strike breaking may be explained by the huge shock to senior Board confidence that the action represented. Not only had the Board not believed that it was going to take place, but a spokesman had gone public with a declaration that supplies were secure. Personnel executives, conscious of the damage to their authority from their failure to predict the action, may have regarded an immediate switch to the Labour Court as a quicker route to settlement than the continuing use of the well tried Joint Industrial Council channel.

While corporately ESB management supported the position of the Council, operationally and at a management level it was seeking major reform of the JIC — a limit to the range of cases that went before it and an attempt to withdraw from it in what was regarded as a headline case. Overall, this position led to confusion on the union side and may have been one of the factors contributing to the groundswell of unexpected support for the TEEU early in the action. In short, the unions perceived the Joint Industrial Council framework to be under threat. A decision to pull a separate row with clerical officers out of the Council and a 1988 management document calling for binding arbitration only confirmed their views.

The Dispute Unfolds

Within two hours of the pickets being placed on power stations and other installations on the morning of Monday, 22 April, the ESB was forced to withdraw its earlier "no cuts" statement issued to the media the previous evening. Direct talks between the TEEU and management on the previous Friday had failed to break the impasse and the union had written to the management providing them with numbers of local strike committee members to deal with emergencies during what they described as their "scheduled industrial action". Fraternal letters to the other unions in the Board had been posted on the Wednesday, specifically requesting the honouring of pickets "where and when placed", but giving no greater detail. Management intelligence had failed to pick up the import of the letter and the Chief Executive of the Labour Relations Commission, the country's major dispute resolving body, said he was told by management there would be no need for his intervention over the critical week-end before the pickets were placed. This assertion by the Commission's Chief Executive was later challenged by the Board's Director of Personnel. The Director says he tried twice over the crucial week-end to contact the Chief Executive of the Labour Relations Commission, through a third party, and indeed there is some independent evidence of this. He also telephoned John Loughrey, Secretary of the Department of Energy, and Kevin Murphy, Secretary for Public Service Management at the Department of Finance. Even if the Commission had been notified earlier, or had chosen to intervene itself, it is by no means certain it could have headed-off the action.

The Minister for Labour of the day, Bertie Ahern, said that one of his officials was told on the Friday "that there was no danger of power cuts for at least a week" (*Irish Independent*, 26 April 1991). The Minister was in his Dublin office on the Saturday night but no one had tried to contact him. Some effort had been made to contact an official on the Sunday, less than 24 hours before picketing began. Media reports based on non-attributable union briefings also spoke of the likelihood of a strike. One senior personnel executive however briefed senior Department of Finance officials, as part of an ongoing reporting relationship, on the possibility of a strike about a week before it began. But it is unlikely it would have been relayed from this quarter to the dispute resolving agencies.

Whatever about the sequence of the events, the Personnel Directorate's handling of the dispute was based on some major miscalculations, not least, failure of the function to detect the rising IR temperature of the organisation. At the time there were a range of items on the bargaining agenda on which little or no progress had been made. This surfaced in the form of delays and complacency in dealing with claims; efforts at decentralisation had also not worked. The Personnel Directorate had effectively operated the hard line that it had maintained on handling claims throughout the 1980s in the run-up to the dispute. And when the dispute broke, it continued this stance despite large numbers of staff — about 80 per cent — observing the picket of a generally unpopular union whose members had previously passed other workers' pickets.

Allegations have been made that the Director of Personnel appears to have been indifferent to the threat posed by the TEEU, despite the fact that it followed the internal procedures to the letter of its agreements with the ESB. ESB management later accepted that the seriousness of the imminent action was not adequately anticipated or conveyed in good time. His efforts to defuse the dispute once it had started were inconsistent, although it has to be said that the room for manoeuvre was limited by virtue of the position he was effectively thrown into; that of the sole defender of the newly signed Programme for Economic and Social Progress (PESP). Given that one of the contributory factors to the dispute was the perception that the Board's internal machinery was under threat, the Director's decision to demand the intervention of the Labour Court in the middle of the dispute is difficult to understand. The Director believed that the national significance of the strike, required a national forum to resolve it, where proceedings would be visible to all. Like the other decisions taken by the Director during the dispute, they had the support of an internal management strategy group and as such were the outcome of a collegiate decision making process.

But management were not alone in making the assumption that the action would not take hold immediately. Management had calculated on about 2,000 people not going to work but on other staff reporting normally. The first notice that the largest union in the Board, the ATGWU received about definite strike action came in a fax on the Saturday at 11.00 am. This union, at official level at any rate, took a clear view of what the TEEU had been trying to achieve by not informing other unions of the timing of their plans: they believed that the electricians had effectively locked everyone else's members out and that there should have been a ballot. The sheer phalanx of support across almost all categories and groups and from staff areas not generally disposed to such actions surprised many: one union leader noted that they had difficulty keeping some vital staff in. Backing from other groups even extended to head office where only four or five electricians actually worked. Overall about two thirds of the Board's staff or about 7,000 were estimated to have stayed out of work, with the strike hitting hardest in generation where all the major groups stayed out with the exception of engineers and shift workers. The official Central Statistics Office (1991) figure for the numbers involved was 6,069.

But the reaction of some disbelief from other unions was nothing as compared to the public outcry over the dispute, partially fuelled by the ESB's very public prediction that it was not going to happen. Confronted by an angry public and hostile press coverage, executives were put on the defensive about the ESB's handling of the row from the outset, barely getting time to get into their stride about the justice or otherwise of the TEEU's case. It was to be the beginning of a very bruising attack on ESB management, with senior personnel executives in the front line taking most of the heat and public frustration.

The media coverage of the strike was extensive with local radio stations ignoring the industrial relations niceties of the peace efforts and concentrating instead on the effects of the cuts on families, farmers and industry. All the national newspapers devoted three and four pages daily to the impact of the dispute, even by the standards of previous ESB disputes, the level of media attention was unprecedented. Radio programmes were used as never before by the chief protagonists, principally the TEEU, to push their case, often is a very partisan fashion. This high level of exposure only served to heighten the public mood over the action but was to feature for the whole duration of the dispute.

The Irish Farmers' Association warned the Government that if "reason did not prevail" within 24 hours it would have no option but to put army engineers into power stations (*Irish Independent*, 24 April 1991). The Confederation of Irish Industry (CII), which later became IBEC, the Irish Business and Employers Confederation, pointed out that such major firms as A T Cross in Ballinasloe, which employed 300 and Fruit of the Loom in Donegal which employed 2,000, were forced to send staff home while workers in other firms were asked to work split shifts to maintain production in off peak periods. In all about 5,000 had to be laid off, it estimated (*Irish Times*, 27 April 1991). The lack of adequate warning about the cuts only fuelled the ferocity of the public reaction. The correctness or otherwise of the ESB's response to the original TEEU claim fell into the background, as did the significance of their stand in national pay bargaining terms. The ESB's lack of notice of the dispute, and the fact that it was occurring at all in troubled economic times, only further encouraged the public's sense of disbelief. The Army had contingency plans to operate power stations in the event of a full blackout and the absence of the interconnector to the North to relieve the situation was also highlighted. However no more than 35 qualified engineers could be provided by the Army Corps of Engineers (*Irish Independent*, 25 April 1991). The ability of the ESB to share the dwindling power supplies equitably was hampered by the fact that switching would normally be carried out by TEEU members who were on the picket lines.

By 9.30 am on the Monday of the week of the strike the ESB

was warning the public of power cuts within 24 hours just as the Labour Relations Commission was trying to convene "talks about talks". The five Midland power stations and Ardnacrusha closed immediately because of the support of other workers and a question mark hung over Moneypoint and Tarbert continuing to supply the grid. By late night supplies from the 915 megawatt Moneypoint coal fired station in Co. Clare, the largest in the country, had ceased and the ESB was predicting its normal 2,000 megawatt output being cut to just 1,200 megawatt by the following morning. The striking electricians had gained more support than they had bargained for from other groups of workers, probably because of the separate agendas they were pursuing against management with little progress. Not only were the power cuts to be more severe than planned but rapid action had to be taken to stop them sinking too low. To avoid output sinking below the "Blue Alert" or about 1,100 megawatts, the level below which chaos on a major scale could not have been avoided, it was decided to allow key workers to boost supply up to the 1400 megawatt level. In fact in its public statement the TEEU had specified minimum output level to be maintained from six key stations (TEEU statement, 22 April 1991). Advice from other unions to members to stay at their posts, but not to carry out work normally done by the TEEU, was ignored. On the evening of the first day of the strike, the Labour Relations Commission held separate talks with the ESB and the TEEU to establish the facts and the issues involved in the dispute. The TEEU proposed that one further local meeting should take place with the ESB. Management however felt that the LRC itself was the appropriate forum for a settlement.

The Labour Relations Commission found a wide gap between both sides but arranged for talks to resume with a senior industrial relations officer the following day. However, the Commission was in a difficult position in what was to be its first major dispute since its inception the previous January. Firstly, it was dealing with a dispute in a company with its own independent industrial relations framework, the outcome of which the TEEU had decisively rejected. It was also faced with a claim which was a direct breach of the three month old PESP which it was expected, by Government, the employers and the unions to uphold.

The second day of the dispute, Tuesday, 23 April, was marked by the first Government statement on the strike, as its widespread effects took hold on the ground with companies laying off staff, cutting back on production and issuing protective notices. By 9.00

am the Board had "shed" about 600 megawatts of demand, plunging thousands of homes into darkness and failing to meet about one-third of peak morning demand. Cuts were of between three and six hours duration, and the huge level of support on the ground prevented planned or scheduled load shedding. Switching was being carried out by engineers rather than electricians who faced an imbalance in generation, with only 20 per cent of generation in Dublin to cater for what was effectively 60 per cent of the national load. ESB was asking its 1.25 million customers to cut demand to conserve dwindling supplies.

The Government's statement following the Tuesday Cabinet meeting expressed "extreme concern" at the strike so soon after the agreement on a new national programme, the PESP (Government Information Services, 23 April 1991). In line with the main recommendation of the Fogarty report, 23 years earlier, it noted that the interest of the country and its people could not be allowed to take second place to the interests of any one group of workers when there were procedures to enable their grievances to be considered. It backed up this firm line by identifying the PESP dimension to the row, stating that the provisions of the deal must be adhered to. The ESB formally referred the row to the Commission. After all night talks on Wednesday morning the ESB suggested to the TEEU that they should accept the outcome of the Joint Industrial Council's deliberations on their case which would allow for their original five per cent claim to be handled within the ambit of the PESP. This would have brought the gap between both sides within the realm of current or future productivity and allowed the TEEU claim to be dealt with under clause three or the local bargaining clause of the PESP. The TEEU response was that they had already conceded productivity and that the PESP clause had nothing to do with its claim which in their eyes had pre-dated the new agreement. While the management of the ESB had formally referred the row to the Commission, the TEEU wanted them to appoint a chairman for talks.

The Fitters' Offer

By this midway stage of the strike, the public airing of the other offers to groups in the ESB, especially fitters, who had been offered a five per cent rise and a £10,000 lump sum, raised eyebrows in the Department of Finance who were unaware of such figures. This offer, however, had not emerged through the standard industrial relations channels, but as noted earlier was part of a sepa-

rate initiative aimed at breaking the log jam in the collective bargaining system. The TEEU was able to point out that while they
were being offered a lump sum for ongoing change, the craft unions, who were also having their agreements reviewed, were being
offered fixed amounts or percentage increases. The fitters offer
was in fact later rejected without being formally introduced. The
Personnel Department were put on the defensive on an offer they
had in fact opposed and which had clearly fuelled the mood for action among the electricians. The break out of the strike resulted in
the Department of Finance seeking a moratorium on so called
category talks with all the groups. The ESB Chief Executive and
the Director of Personnel were asked to go to the Department of
Finance at a meeting to establish the Board's position on safe-
guarding the PESP.

Thursday, 25 April, was the day the now three day old effort by
the Labour Relations Commission for peace was to collapse, pav-
ing the way for a reference back to the Joint Industrial Council by
the TEEU. It was also to mark new and more heightened Government concern at the delay in getting a resolution, with the
Taoiseach telling the Dáil that "further measures were being considered", a hint of stronger action if a solution were not found.
Significantly, this was the cue for the ICTU and its general secretary Peter Cassells to enter the picture — from the sidelines at
first.

Adding to rising tension was a warning from an eminent senior
counsel that the striking electricians could face legal action over
the disruption of supplies under a little known section of the 1927
Act which set up the ESB. Michael McDowell SC wrote that:

> The Electricity Supply Act provided in section 110 that the le-
> gal ban on strikes affecting water and gas supplies should be
> extended to the to the provision of electricity for the ESB (*Irish
> Independent*, 26 April 1991).

The talks at the Commission finally broke down later that afternoon with the TEEU, as hinted earlier in the week, unilaterally
referring the dispute back to the Joint Industrial Council. The
Commission had been conscious of the need to get the dispute
back to the forum where it had started, and not to risk taking any
move which might have damaged the ESB's own internal machinery or the integrity of the original Council recommendation. The
Joint Industrial Council meeting commenced around 5.00 pm
about two hours after discussions had broken down at the LRC

with the council chairman running the proceedings. The ESB publicly stated that it was not optimistic about a settlement.

The Joint Industrial Council's Commentary

Around 3.30 am on the morning of Friday 26 April, hopes for a settlement rose sharply when the Joint Industrial Council issued a statement. Caught between not wanting to unravel its own earlier recommendation and yet play a positive part in the strike resolution, the Council issued a commentary which stated that "in the interests of all concerned it would be best if the industrial action was called off to allow negotiations to proceed in an expeditious way".

The JIC Chairman's comment that the Council believed that its recommendation would be acceptable to both sides clearly suggested that it carried the weight of all parties in the nightlong talks, including the management and the TEEU representatives. But within five hours, any such understanding publicly fell apart as a union spokesman, also a worker director, went on radio to demand unconditional talks before any return to work. His comments followed the ESB's acceptance of the formula. It had agreed to talks on the broader agenda including productivity, no doubt primed by the then Labour Minister still operating in the background. The change in position appears to have been cemented by some figures within the TEEU wanting to adopt a harder stance than the understanding the union had sanctioned during the emergency talks at the JIC behind closed doors. In the eyes of those involved in the Joint Industrial Council talks from all sides, the process had effectively been derailed. The JIC had proposed a resumption of work and then talks; the publicly expressed TEEU position was for talks prior to any resumption. This was the direct opposite to the agreed intent by all sides during the night.

Talks resumed that Friday afternoon at the Department of Labour with Minister for Labour Bertie Ahern actively involved. At around 3.55 am the Minister accompanied by his advisers announced that the strike was finally over while staying within the terms of the original Joint Industrial Council recommendation. The striking TEEU were to get an ongoing payment of £10 a week for a period of 65 weeks with further talks to take place about making it permanent in return for new productivity. The solution was based on proposals put forward by his Department and the ICTU. The formula was in fact a slight redrafting of the pay terms of the original JIC document and amounted to paying the £650 lump sum in a different form, i.e. paying £10 a week over 65 weeks. In effect, it expressed the same pay terms in a different way. The only difference was that they were being paid the rise in the form of an ongoing payment instead of a lump sum, thus meeting one of their key demands that any rise be ongoing. The intention was that during the 65 weeks talks would take place on further new productivity measures which would allow for the continued payment of the £10 indefinitely. In the end, it took another three years to reach final agreement with the 1,000 electricians on a six per cent productivity agreement. It was finally concluded in June 1994.

The hectic round of talks and their failure to produce a solution until the eleventh hour forced the Government into considering drastic measures, according to central figures in the discussions later. The device most talked about was the legal enforcement of the original JIC recommendation, the rejection of which led to the dispute. Settlement, however, made this radical step unnecessary.

Management Strategy and the Outcome of the Dispute

The Personnel Department of the ESB launched into the resolution of the 1991 dispute in a mood of no little consternation. The belief that the action was not going to threaten supplies was based on past experience of previous disputes and the custom and practice that had surrounded past rows, particularly the use of the 48 hour picketing rule. The severity and speed at which supplies were cut only added to the shock that had been experienced by those who did not believe the strike was going to happen, especially the Director of Personnel. But having seen the TEEU claim go through procedures and the Joint Industrial Council, the initial management position once the strike began was to stand by the procedures and the outcome of its own machinery. Having resisted the TEEU's claim as unreasonable in negotiations, principally on the grounds that it represented a demand for past productivity, personnel management operated the Fogarty dictum of standing up to unfair demands. When the row went public, personnel were left in the position of having to demand adherence by the TEEU to the outcome of the JIC procedures, a process they themselves had wished to abandon two years earlier. In effect, the Directorate were forced into the position of defending a system whose continuing suitability in the ESB context they had seriously questioned. The Joint Industrial Council process was perceived to be under threat by the unions and this was a contributory factor to the

strike. The public call for a Labour Court role in the strike's resolution just tended to confirm the belief that the Council's future
was at risk. When the dispute was eventually settled at 4.00 am
on Saturday, 26 April, 1991 in the Minister's city centre Departmental offices, he was asked his view on how it was handled:

> I do not want to criticise anyone but I have seen disputes han-
> dled far better (IRN, 7, 1991).

At a macro level the strike, coming as it did three months after the
signing of the Programme for Economic and Social Progress
(PESP), resulted in ESB management being pushed into the position of having to defend the pay limits contained in the deal. In its
statement on the second day of the strike, the Government clearly
painted the action as a threat to the newly signed national agreement and warned that its provisions must be adhered to
(Government Information Services, 23 April 1991). The management had gone "to the brink" as they had done with many of the
disputes of the late 1980s and operated to the Fogarty principle of
standing up to unreasonable demands. Roche and Brannick (1987)
noted the way in which the economic climate within the Board had
"hardened" during this period. This had resulted in a "tougher
stance on negotiations and the conduct of industrial relations
more generally".

TABLE 5.1:
WORKING DAYS LOST PER 100 EMPLOYEES, 1960-91

Year	Civilian Employees at Work (average)	ESB Workforce (average)
1960/69	62	199
1970/79	79	24
1980/84	51	84
1985/91	20	144

Source: Dues Projects & Strikes Project Files. Department of Industrial
Relations, UCD.

Table 5.1 shows the levels of working days lost in the Board
over three decades compared to the average for civilian employees.
Overall, the 1970s saw a drop in days lost after the Fogarty rules
were introduced. The 1980s saw an increase and this was sustained into the 1990s through the strike. The outcome of the 1991

dispute resulted in an open questioning of the Fogarty strategy of standing up to strikes. Not only had the dispute challenged the existing personnel orthodoxy, but it threw into question the second pillar of the Fogarty strategy which the Board had operated in all major rows. The issues at stake in the 1991 dispute were no less momentous than those envisaged by Fogarty but whatever about Government support, community support never emerged. Instead, the hostility directed at the Board from all quarters led one senior figure to believe that:

> The top management of the company are now ad idem in the view that if we have another serious strike involving power cuts, we might as well all resign. The public will not just put up with it. But this gives a signal to staff.

In terms of the outcome of the dispute vis a vis existing personnel strategy, the outcome was to mark a sea change in management thinking, the roots of which had been laid some years earlier by the New Generation initiative. As one senior figure with close experience of developments during the late 1980s and the rise of HRM thinking noted:

> There was an outcome in terms of IR strategy. We would wish to get to a stage where IR has its own part in the relationship with people and managers. IR had become quite pervasive but there are many things that are not part of it and are part of relationships. But management failed to take them into another arena.

At one level this amounted to a weakening of the position of those who presided over the conduct of industrial relations along the lines of the traditional model. While the input from personnel still had a role, in future it would be a smaller element in a bigger jigsaw whose shape would be determined well outside its control.

Transformative Impact

The 1991 strike brought to the surface major weaknesses in the ESB's system of collective bargaining which piecemeal reform had failed to address. Initiatives to change the rules of bargaining, and particularly of the Joint Industrial Council, were stymied firstly by top management but also by Government intervention and ultimately union resistance. These conditions produced a policy paralysis within personnel, which reduced not only its leverage but also its ability to respond to crisis situations imaginatively. This clearly emerged in the handling of the strike by the Personnel Directorate. The mood of uncertainty in the run-up to the appointment of a new Chief Executive in March 1991, just a month before the strike, may have contributed to a reluctance to initiate any major policy shifts. Thus, when the strike broke almost unannounced, management's sole position was that the union involved, the Technical, Engineering and Electrical Trade Union (TEEU), adhere to procedures and accept the Joint Industrial Council recommendation. This had emerged from a process in which they themselves had less than total faith or confidence.

Management's policy of accepting every Council recommendation provides them with a moral authority, executives argue. But it also removes their bargaining power, leaves them dependent on one policy lever and closes off other back channels of communication. It also creates an essential imbalance in the bargaining relationship across the table which is underpinned by the Board's monopoly on the supply of electricity. Management may have felt entitled to adopt a tough policy with issues outside the Council in view of its predictable acceptance of every recommendation within it.

The failure by the Personnel Directorate to detect that the strike was about to break, or communicate publicly the immediacy of the threat to supplies, seriously undermined its authority and contributed to transformation. The myriad of unresolved issues the dispute itself exposed and the handling of the strike only added to this momentum. The public outcry over the strike and the inadequacy of the ESB response to achieve a resolution has had major consequences. Traditional collective bargaining mechanisms are no longer regarded as the principle vehicle for the handling of employee relations issues. In this context the role of industrial relations is being downplayed as unions and management explore alternative human resource management options, including worker participation in decision-making and the generation of trust. Collective bargaining in the ESB has contributed to its own demise by its failure to reform itself. This is attributable to lack of competition, "over internalisation" of IR issues underpinned by political intervention and management's lack of an alternative strategy.

Conclusion

Beer and Spector (1985: 238) note that only when "pressures from the competitive environment or from the workforce mesh with top leadership support for change will HRM transformations acceler-ate and begin to encompass the whole organisation". In the case of the ESB, a perceived threat to the future of the organisation from the Government in the wake of the strike, its possible break-up allied to the crisis of pluralism and EC directives provided the stimulus. Top management in the ESB moved within weeks of the settlement of the dispute to utilise the "window of opportunity" created by the crisis of pluralism to mould a new working model based on partnership. The unions also moved, but for reasons more linked to their own survival, onto a new agenda for change, which they were able to share with management.

Both these initiatives — the McKinsey proposals for restructur-ing the company into Separate Business Units and the Cassells Review of Relationships report — are explored in detail in the next chapter which seeks to asses their implications for the future shape of employee relations in the Board and for each other. Both these initiatives represent the transformation of the "internal ground rules" in the Board in the internal/external definition of the dynamics of transformation disputes developed in Chapter Three. But this transformation is by no means complete and, as will be discussed in the next chapter, is facing its greatest test to date with new demands for radical changes in work practices and 2,900 job cuts, which were tabled in late September 1994 by McKinsey consultants.

Chapter Seven

NEW STRATEGIES FOR CHANGE IN THE ESB

Introduction

The crisis produced by the 1991 dispute altered the balance and agenda of employee relations in the ESB — but not in the way intended by either side before the strike, nor in the way outlined by most of the literature on post-traumatic developments. The net effect of the British miners' dispute of 1984/5, as we have seen, was to marginalise the National Union of Mineworkers (NUM), both centrally and locally, while pushing up productivity (Edwards and Heery, 1989). But the unique micro-political climate of ESB industrial relations was to produce a very different result. The most important outcome of the 1991 ESB strike from the unions' point of view was that it put an end to the "no give policy" of the 1980s and at direct efforts to reduce their power and influence. The 1991 Employee Relations Handbook for negotiators (1991: 4) listed "the reduction in the effectiveness of trade union power" as one of the Board's central objectives; the 1993 Employee Relations Handbook substituted "union commitment to acceptance of change" in its place (1993: 5).

The transformation effected by the strike produced a highly complicated set of outcomes in personnel terms with differing long-term consequences. The process was accelerated by a Government proposal to break the Board into two separate companies responsible for generation and transmission, first raised by the Minister for Energy, Robert Molloy, ten months after the strike in February 1992 (*Irish Independent* and *Irish Times*, 8 February 1992). A change of Government, and a new Minister for Energy, following a general election in late 1992 meant this approach was reviewed by the incoming administration.

After a major public humiliation of management because of the strike's crippling impact, the nerve and confidence of many senior executives and of the organisation itself was shattered. In time, three different sets of operational imperatives, with specific tensions and conflicts between them, emerged. All three strands of emerging policy — the Cassells Report on Relationships, the McKinsey Corporate Review restructuring plan and the maintenance of the existing pluralistic collective bargaining machinery — are circumscribed by a range of Government policies which severely limit their strategic potential. The Cassells and McKinsey initiatives, which will be explored in this chapter, form the main modes of internal transformation which arose from the 1991 dispute.

From a management perspective, the strike led to a major change of strategy and ultimately to the sanctioning of the biggest structural change in the company since 1927. The dispute resulted in management switching their strategy from a partial implementation of human resource management in generation and the standard industrial relations model throughout the rest of the company, to an overall HRM policy with strong dualist characteristics. Ironically, a dispute from which the electricians gained nothing in monetary terms has given the unions a greater say over a wider range of issues, including those outside the traditional industrial relations ambit, while at the same time allowing management to make a major strategy change. It can be argued that the outcome provided a lifeline to the unions, while at the same time granting management a new platform for change, much of it linked to EU moves on deregulation of the electricity industry.

The immediate aftermath of the strike cast doubts over the future role and influence of the Personnel Directorate, which had supervised the internal IR system and the policy of reducing union power. The reputation and credibility of the function suffered a serious blow in the wake of the strike, partly because of its miscalculation over timing, but also because of a myriad of deadlocked and unfinished business the dispute exposed. While the general body of personnel staff face decentralisation to the five new ESB divisions, which will each have their own personnel function, the Director of Personnel has assumed a new post in the central hierarchy. As Corporate Personnel Director, his function will be to assess the personnel impact of plans, establish policy and monitor compliance to the new "soft" HRM policy being pursued. Thus, while the policy has changed, the figures leading it have remained in place. This contrasts with the changes within generation, where the Director of Generation has a new post outside the area and the new Managing Director of Power Generation has moved over from heading the distribution business.

This chapter seeks to describe and analyse in both theoretical and practical terms the major initiatives launched by management in the wake of the 1991 dispute, in particular the Corporate Review/McKinsey Report and the Cassells Committee Report into Relationships. Both initiatives can be regarded, at one level, as damage limitation exercises; Cassells being launched to avoid a more critical external review and McKinsey as a submission to a Government-commissioned consultant's study on splitting the ESB. While the Corporate Review of which McKinsey was a major part had commenced before the strike, its conclusions were clearly tempered by the dispute outcome; most are agreed its findings would have been more "hard-nosed" if the action had not taken place. Its terms of reference were broadened to take the Government review into account

The strike pinpointed the failure of management and unions in one of the most secure and better paid employments in the country to agree reform in the system of collective bargaining they operated. On the union side, it highlighted the problem of lack of union co-ordination and the failure of the Group of Unions mechanism in the ESB which had been addressed over 20 years earlier by the Fogarty Committee. The 1991 strike exposed a crisis of pluralism in the Board that had been under way for some time. The playing out of these various crises during the strike, in a language that ignored the national imperative of the demand for continuous supplies, ultimately unnerved the Government. In the eyes of many it led to a determination among senior Government officials and some politicians that the conditions under which the 1991 strike had occurred — a monopoly business and over-powerful unions — would not be allowed continue. The 1991 strike, in the view of many union figures and senior ESB staff, changed for the worse the nature of relations between the Board and the Government with lasting impact. One senior figure commented:

> Up to 1991 the ESB was riding high, prices were low and had not been raised for a number of years and our financial situation was good. Suddenly the TEEU situation arose and the strike occurred. It changed the attitude of politicians towards us and showed how vulnerable the country was. They felt we were a State within a State and the time had come to bring it to a halt.

While the question of Government/ESB relations does not fall directly within the ambit of this book — only in so far as it has a bearing on the dynamics of and changes to the Board's industrial relations system — the strike resulted in a more critical and questioning approach at official level. It transformed the external ground rules the company faced, particularly in relation of Government's handling and control of key areas like prices and investment decisions. These issues will be discussed later in the context of their impact on management strategy.

This ability of both management and unions to come together, as in the Cassells Review, to fend off a more robust external examination is probably another example of the sort of tripartite political exchange that is a feature of the relations between the Government, ESB management and its unions. It allows for a re-accommodation between the parties on a new basis in the face of the threat of externally imposed change from the political centre. The key to understanding this set of outcomes is the company's status as a state-owned monopoly producer of power, on which the country is totally dependent. Management and unions came together again early in 1994, in the Cost and Competitiveness Review, to examine costs after the Government indicated it was going to carry out its own separate examination.

The central argument of this book is that the dispute was the catalyst for the transformation process of which these two initiatives were a major part and which is still under way — the Cost and Competitiveness Review (CCR) being the latest instalment. It brought to the surface, and exposed in the most public way, weaknesses in the Board's collective bargaining system that had been identified by line and central management as far back as 1983, and extensively noted, but not immediately responded to. It dramatised in the most public fashion possible and in the gaze of national media attention how the operation of the "no give" policy of the 1980s effectively led management down a policy cul de sac. Within two years, by April 1993, the Government, the unions and the company had accepted an altered structure for the ESB, breaking it into separate business units (SBUs). They had also accepted a new template for the conduct of industrial relations which, while less explicit and more aspirational than Fogarty, had helped "clear the ground" for the new management strategy. These two reports and the structures they recommended have effectively transformed management strategy and to a lesser extent modified staff expectations. But the price of acceptance of this heavily HRM-influenced report was to be the continuation of many of the elements of the older IR system, central to the ESB "claims culture".

Thus the "unfinished business" from the pluralist agenda, including outstanding category claims, all present unique hurdles to be overcome if the new initiatives and restructuring are to be successfully introduced. The plan to cut job numbers in the Board by 2,900 over the next three to five years in response to competitive pressures and continuing Government unease over prices, raises further dilemmas. As much of recent literature on HRM is largely silent on the problems introducing the commitment model into highly unionised and monopolistic environments, some of the pointers will necessarily be speculative. But, on paper at least, running the McKinsey/Separate Business Unit strategy and the later plan for job cuts and work practice changes — with hardnosed aspirations of performance and benchmarking — alongside the Cassells initiative of new relationships and sharing of core values, has the ring of "hard" and "soft" HRM being driven in parallel.

McKinsey Restructuring

The foundations for the McKinsey proposals for the ESB are to be found in the Board's own report, "Connecting with the Future — ESB Strategies for the 1990s" published in March 1990. Containing as it did the views of the Board and management on key strategic issues affecting performance, "Connecting with the Future" was heavily influenced by the same factors which influenced the New Generation Programme (NGP) two years earlier. Key among these were the gradual erosion of surplus capacity and the fact that sustained electricity growth in demand of six per cent for the next 10 years would pose "insurmountable problems for the ESB and the country generally". The internal report favoured pegging growth at around half of this predicted level for a decade and urged the development of marketing strategies to support this approach.

The objectives of the Corporate Management Review undertaken by ESB management and McKinsey Consultants — the terms of which were later broadened to include restructuring options for the industry as a whole — focused on the external trends within the EU. These can be summarised as the creation of full transparency in generation, transmission, distribution and supply activities; supporting competition in generation, including the introduction of independent power producers; and giving customers a greater say, as well as a choice of suppliers, for large users. Greater efficiency was to be encouraged through a more profit-orientated approach and major change was to be achieved in the approach to the management of the ESB. These objectives were similar to those that had guided the restructuring of a number of electricity supply industries in Europe and throughout the world.

The original McKinsey report (1992) recommended that the Irish electricity market should be restructured and that electricity generation should be subject to competition. Any new capacity should be added through an open and competitive process with the existing plant competing once their initial contracts had expired. In terms of regulation, a new Industry Regulator, who would be distanced from industry participants and political pressures alike, would be created. The Regulator would audit the operation of the competitive markets and set broad performance targets for industry players in the light of Government policy. Such a Regulator had been a key element in the success of restructuring in a number of other countries and in particular should help attract private capital.

Four different options were finally evaluated: modify the existing structure to facilitate competition; restructure the ESB into business units; spin off a single generation company and spin off multiple generation companies. The 28 page consultant's report finally backed the "business unit approach" which met a number of the objectives identified by the Corporate Management Review, in particular some key behavioural changes. These were identified as thinking and acting more strategically; executing more effectively — ensuring there was a "bias for action" with clear accountability at all levels and improving the interface with external constituencies, such as the general public, industry groups, the EC, Government and unions. It called for "institutionalising change", that is, establishing a culture and systems that support the process of change, and creating an environment where staff at all levels were motivated and able to participate fully in the development of the business and the provision of quality service.

The ESB would in effect be divided up into five business units covering Generation, Transmission Systems, Customer Services, Ancillary Services and a Central Business Service Unit. The Generation division would be charged with producing bulk power at minimum cost from ESB stations under contracts negotiated with the Power Procurer. Transmission Systems Operations would be responsible for dispatching at arms length, supplies from the generating stations, as well as from independent producers. The Customer Services division would provide open access distribution to all generators and suppliers based on transparent and fair use of systems changes. Supply costs would be separated from distribution costs to ensure transparency and to eliminate any possibility of cross subsidy. Ancillary Activities would constitute the fourth business unit and be responsible for managing the ESB's non-core activities. The Business Services Unit would provide shared services to the other units as well as to the Corporate Centre.

Authority over the business units was to be held by the Chief Executive. The primary interface would be in the setting of planning guidelines and specific targets; the approval of plans and the monitoring of performance against plans and targets. The report estimated that given the new role, the staffing requirement at the Corporate Centre would not exceed between 50 and 80 people. The Chief Executive would be supported by three Corporate Directors with responsibility for corporate strategy and technology, finance and personnel operations who would have only a limited involvement in the business units.

A greater emphasis would be placed on external recruitment, especially at senior management levels. Appointments at senior levels in the company would be used to signal change and inject new experience into the top management. Ironically, when it came to filling the five Chief Executive posts in the Separate Business Units and the four new Director posts, only three of the jobs were advertised. Six of the positions were filled by people in existing senior management positions. Some office holders in the old ESB management structure simply assumed new titles in the Corporate Centre while retaining their existing responsibilities. Senior union figures and others voiced some concern privately over the this practice, fearing it could impact on the creditability of the overall change process with staff. Training and development of staff was already at a high level, but in future greater emphasis would be placed on the development of management skills. The report said that performance evaluation and reward would also be substantially different in future, with performance measures being derived from the business unit targets.

The Cassells Report

The final report of the Joint Steering Committee which carried out a Review of Relationships within the ESB was published in February, 1993 — 18 months after the group was set up. Chaired by

Irish Congress of Trades Unions (ICTU) General Secretary Peter Cassells, it was created in the aftermath of the strike in May 1991 and regarded in some quarters as an effort to fend off the threat of a more critical examination by Government-appointed figures outside the company. The Group consisted of five management and five union representatives with a secretary and a project co-ordinator.

Its terms of reference were to commission and oversee a comprehensive review of relationships, including industrial relations in the ESB; to provide management and the ESB Group of Unions with the report and recommendations of the Review; and to advise what further action, if any, needs to be taken. The Steering Committee was to operate on a consensus basis and not by a majority decision. But it made clear that it did not see its role in terms of analysing the weaknesses or otherwise of the collecting bargaining system that had operated in the ESB since the Fogarty Report was published in 1969.

The Committee divided its exercise into two phases. It hired MORI consultants to carry out a survey of staff attitudes and created five working groups to look at areas like the company's future, relationships, career structures and equality, industrial relations structures and participation and involvement. Its first report, published in July 1992, set out eight key issues that needed to be addressed: the need to develop shared objectives; to build trust; to recognise and foster and aspirations and contribution of individuals; the need to make the industrial relations process more effective; the need to develop a framework for participation; the need to improve communication; the need to develop the roles of both management and the trade unions and how both sides should build on their strengths.

The key recommendations of the report are based on the unquestioned unitarist assumption that both sides can share the same vision of the company. Trade unions representatives told the Committee (1993: 13), in words not normally associated with collective bargaining, that "attempting to implement change in the absence of a shared vision forces them into a reactive role". The report also notes that "acceptance of company objectives by staff and unions requires that staff have a meaningful input to those objectives".

The initial survey data for the Committee revealed that 68 per cent of staff felt there was a lack of trust in relations while 70 per cent believed the management to be "out of touch". Seventy-six per cent said that management was more interested in giving information than listening to the views of others.

Based on its deliberations, and with the help of outside consultants, the Joint Steering Committee produced a vision for the future of an ESB "which is noted for excellence in everything it does and in particular for the quality of relationships between all its people" (1993: 12). It believed that the only means of achieving peace and progress towards that vision was through partnership and co-operation between management, staff and unions. The "legitimate and fundamental role and contribution of management, staff and unions" was to be clearly understood and accepted by all. The three groups were to share understanding and acceptance of the need to work together constructively in partnership to achieve progress and success in a peaceful environment. Conflicts of interest will be dealt with through an industrial relations system which enables issues to be resolved peacefully and expeditiously through discussion and negotiation.

It then outlined its blueprint for the future under the headings of Contributions and Aspirations of Individuals; Equal Opportunities for Women; Roles of Unions and Management; Participation and Involvement, and Communication. Having largely ignored the collective bargaining genesis of the 1991 dispute, the report examined industrial relations in the Board, not in their real-life context but in terms of how they would fit into the newly constructed relationship and the partnership model. And where the reality of the previous 10 years seeped through, even in coded form, it was presented in terms of strong vested interests on both sides more interested in maintaining the existing approach.

The report presented different elements of ESB industrial relations machinery, but separated them from their context and recent operating histories. It called for ESB management and the newly reconstituted Group of Unions to develop a new understanding of the role of industrial relations processes in the changing business environment of the 1990s. This would include examining industrial relations procedures and processes appropriate to the structure and the competitive needs of the ESB as well as conciliation. The role and operation of the Joint Industrial Council would also be examined. Guidelines were also to be drawn up about the appropriate level at which different issues should be handled, in order to avoid undue or unnecessary submissions to central level. This section of the report also proposed that there should be formal and regular consultations between managers and union representatives in a non-confrontational setting on matters of mutual concern. At corporate level, top management and senior representatives of the reconstituted Group of Unions should meet at least twice yearly in the new Corporate Forum. At local level, line managers, including station managers and branch managers, should meet once a quarter.

The Committee recognised the need for more clear-cut and rational trade union representation in the ESB in which the Group of Unions would be the authoritative body operating to the highest professional standards. The report also noted that the present culture of the ESB presents obstacles to the achievement of a generally participative organisation. On the role of worker directors, the committee noted concern about their involvement in industrial relations matters. It stressed that there appeared to be a "lack of clarity" surrounding aspects of their role which should be addressed. This particular recommendation arose from some worker directors taking front line responsibilities for ongoing IR issues. This came to a head with one worker director becoming the public spokesman for the striking electricians during the actual dispute, appearing almost daily on television and radio putting forward their public position with some success. So called "institutionalised overtime" of 12 days for shift operatives was to end and payments above basic pay, such as duty money and shift premia were to be discontinued with basic payments only.

The 1994 Cost and Competitiveness Review Proposals

The Cost and Competitiveness Review (CCR) grew out of a proposal by the Minister for Transport, Energy and Communications, Brian Cowen, to employ consultants to carry out a detailed review of the ESB's costs to see how they compared with best international practice. The Government decided to defer any decision on the long-standing 1992 price application until this was completed. Following discussions between the Chief Executive and the ESB Group of Unions in early 1994, a counter proposal was put to the Minister for a tripartite study, in the spirit of the Cassells Review. But the unions and management had been considering their own study prior to the Minister's announcement.

The CCR set out to examine all aspects of ESB's operations, including the utilisation of existing assets, the capital expenditure programme, operating expenditure, financial charges and social levies. Teams of management and union officials visited power station and supply facilities abroad to see how they organised their activities, the work methods employed and the results achieved. The teams recorded what they saw with the help of McKinsey consultants and a plan which embodied the best practices from the different operations was drawn up. Proposals which emerged in September 1994 sought a reduction of 2,900 jobs over five years —half of which would go in generation — major changes in work practices and management de-layering. Overtime levels were to be cut from 18 per cent to 8 per cent, the costs of routine maintenance were to be reduced and more extensive use was to be made of outside contractors, particularly in power stations (IRN, 37, 1994). New flexible working was to be introduced under which transmission staff would work four ten hour days; two man crews were to be brought in, and in generation operations staff were to carry out minor maintenance and help clean plants. In addition, as part of the overall cost savings plan, aimed at saving over £100 million, 35 area offices were to be closed, a demand that is likely to be politically sensitive.

The CCR proposals basically built on what was in the 1992 McKinsey review, but elaborated on many of the proposals and made concrete suggestions on their implementation, based on best industry practice. Like the original McKinsey package in 1992, the new proposals were influenced by European deregulation and new competitive pressures. The entire package is now the subject of negotiations with the trade unions in the company. Unlocking existing agreements, rather than securing redundancies, will be the key to its success. But the initial trade union reaction was one of calm, after some early conditioning on the outcome. But the discussions will face major obstacles in the final stages, particularly in relation to manning and new work practices, and the issue of an overall "wrap-up" category deal for all those who remain in the new situation.

Assessing McKinsey

The McKinsey model for the ESB owes much of its shape to the thinking outlined in the Board's own internal document, "Connecting to the Future", which addressed the strategic issues of demand, plant availability and investment. But this document talked mainly of structures and said little about the processes for managing employees beyond emphasising the need for high quality training and development programmes. It noted that some companies had reorganised around a core of critical business activities and contracted out all peripheral tasks. McKinsey, on the other hand, was much more explicit and was peppered with references to the behavioural changes needed and demanded a "vision led change process" allied to the major changes in structures and goal setting. It linked with the Review of Relationships Committee and talked of creating an environment where "staff at all levels were motivated and able to participate fully in the development of the business and the provision of quality service to customers" (McKinsey, 1992: 19).

The intention was that Personnel or HR policy would be determined at the centre, and further developed in the satellites, depending on culture and business conditions. But, according to a figure charged with drawing up the new Personnel policy in the new Corporate centre, the implementation will mean:

> The human resources strategies will be put in place to support the business and not the other way around. The HR management should be a facilitation to achieve the objectives of this company and to achieve what is most consistent with the commitment and involvement of staff.

But it would be less prescriptive. So while the overall approach would be to introduce the best of human resource management, local management and local personnel directors would have some latitude as to application and usage. The division into Separate Business Units (SBUs), as noted by Storey (1992) and other writers, and the creation of "mini businesses", have often been linked to the spread of excellence and changing corporate cultures. As a set of inter-locking principles and processes, HRM has been concerned with the rise of competition and the freeing up of management initiative.

Internal And External Fit

The McKinsey document (1992: 27) talked of the "linkage of personal performance goals to business goals". In other words, it sought to reflect external market and competition conditions internally in regard to pay rates, structure and style of management, and in particular to measuring individual performance. But other parts of the report talked of a more soft-focused approach involving participation, commitment and vision. And the Cassells report, whose conclusions and thinking as we will see later fed into the McKinsey process, develop this thinking even further through the need to build trust and common cause, creating a system where openness and frankness were core values. This apparent contradiction, between a hard nosed business policy and a "soft" HRM strategy, can be encapsulated into the concept of tough love. ESB executives have talked about the future in a similar vein, stressing respect for the individual and the need for commitment alongside the reality that many managers and other staff who cannot relate to the new environment will have to be "dispensed with". The contradictions and conflicts that arise in operating a soft HRM policy alongside an existing centralised collectivist system will be considered later when assessing the overall Cassells approach.

The type of HRM approach highlighted by McKinsey ignores or is silent on the political context within which Irish semi-state companies operate, particularly in regard to pay and prices. Both these variables are highly controlled in the ESB context, and the way they operate in the micro political climate of the ESB/Government/Union relations has a huge bearing on relations with staff. As we have already seen, ESB management partly fought the 1991 strike as a defender of national pay norms. More critical to its strategic role under the HRM model, management does not have the freedom to award pay rises in isolation. Tight Government directives on pay means that management's discretion in this crucial area is severely restricted. Paradoxically, the Board's ability to recruit new management blood, to oversee and implement the sort of change outlined by McKinsey has been severely hampered by the existence of the so-called Gleeson pay guidelines, according to senior executives. Such pay limits on remuneration for senior public sector executives have resulted in a big gap opening up between private and public sector salaries in Ireland, particularly at the highest executive level. The politically sensitive nature of price rises — the Board lodged an application for a "price contract" in April 1992 for its first increase since 1986 — means that a second management freedom under the HRM model does not really apply in the Irish context. Apart from the difficulty of introducing HRM in a highly unionised environment, which we shall look at later, these constraints challenge some of the core values of textbook HRM, such as management's ability to make strategic decisions across all areas of the business and its ability to integrate all policies. It simply does not have access to the levers of control in regard to these two key areas.

Laying the Dualist Foundations

While the impetus for the Fogarty investigation into ESB in 1968 came from the Government, the roots of the Cassells report emerged from within the Board itself. The original idea to set up the Cassells group in 1991 emerged within a week of the ending of the strike as part of an overall management response to the crisis, other parts of which included an assessment of the issues involved and reassuring staff and customers. By setting up a group composed of management and unions working to a remit agreed within the ESB, senior executives were dealing with several issues at once. At one level it was a damage limitation exercise to avoid a more critical external examination of the workings of the ESB.

The decision to focus on an "overall review of relationships including industrial relations" and to operate on a consensus basis, set the tone for the report. The notion of industrial relations as a sub-set of a wider relationship between management and unions had gained little currency in the more adversarial 1980s in the Board. Adopting the wider canvas inevitably skewed the orientation of the group more towards the future than to the past. Its criticisms were implicit rather than explicit, and its analysis of the past was so heavily coded and lacking in the strength of the major events as to render it meaningless to all but the initiated. But it did provide room for people to modify and develop their positions, albeit within a wider human resource/employee relations frame. As a model of the future it barely met Walton's criteria for a model as a "general concept of the future organisation that evolves from the understanding of limitations of traditional understanding and experimentation with alternatives".

By imposing a language and an orientation which was not part of the normal IR relationship or discourse, the group at once distanced themselves from the events of the past and, in a sense, removed themselves from responsibility for it. What emerges in the report is a mixture of heavily HRM-influenced thinking to put employee relations on a new plane, where participation and trust play a major role, alongside a desire to keep the existing industrial relations system largely intact, but subjecting it to a review in the wider knowledge of recent events. This "dualist" approach, which is now effectively the dominant policy of the ESB personnel function, was itself, it appears, the result of an internal accommodation within the Cassells group, which was composed equally of management and union representatives. As one figure associated with the process put it:

The price of Cassells signing up for HRM was to leave existing machinery in situ. I do not think that the Cassells committee took a sufficiently hard look at IR as a means of doing business. It was starting out with certain givens; that IR is a legitimate way of mediating the differences between management and unions. A sophisticated HRM approach would question that.

The Cassells' document sought to place the ICTU in somewhat of a policing role vis a vis the ESB unions — one they are likely to strenuously resist. The emphasis was on developing a culture of trust and change and the creation of a new process.

Assessing the impact of maintaining a collective bargaining regime alongside a HRM style participation/trust and commitment model is more difficult. The literature highlights that one of the most notable results is likely to be less emphasis upon achieving productivity gains through the existing mechanisms and machinery. There are already firm indications that ESB management wants to jettison the "pay for change era" as soon as practicable with the key issue being how do you close down existing agreements in the context of the creation of new subdivisions and further demands for change. Storey (1992: 257) points out that the overall impact of the new emphasis on individualistic human resource style policies on trade unions, collective bargaining and industrial relations was hard to gauge. But traditional pay struggles tended to continue.

Other writers, including Cradden (1992), have tried to define a brand of human resource management that can co-exist with trade unions. He tries to resolve the apparent contradictions between pluralism and individualist HRM by stressing the possibilities of "dual allegiance". Like Kochan et al (1986) he highlights examples of where "soft" HRM drivers were installed into unionised environments with some success, but cautions that these were often single union sites. But most of these "dualist" strategies were driven in free market, post-crisis situations where unions did not have the monopoly power they enjoy in the ESB. In short, they had less to lose.

Implications of "Double Dualism"

Introducing the parallel and sometimes clashing strategies of McKinsey and Cassells into the ESB represents a major challenge, not only to unions and management but to the embedded IR "claims" culture of the organisation. The Cassells report attempts

to overlay a trust, commitment and participation model of relationships on top of the largely unreformed industrial relations su-
perstructure which produced the 1991 dispute. Thus, there is an
inherent conflict or difference of emphasis within the Cassells
model between the heavily proceduralised, power-broking industrial relations system, that is the bedrock of ESB, and the aspiration to a shared view of the future which is the central theme of
the report. In parallel, the McKinsey plan to subdivide the ESB
into five new divisions, including generation, demands adherence
to a range of new performance criteria, including benchmarking to
international standards, which will put the improved relationships envisaged by Cassells under severe strain. Achieving both
sets of ambitions simultaneously will present major pitfalls for
both sides, but particularly for management. A clear conflict exists
between the sort of consensual approach to every issue espoused
by Cassells, with up to seven stages in the decision making process, and the almost immediate change demands sought by McKinsey in the context of the opening up of generation to competition
and independent power producers.

The applicability of a free market HRM model to the ESB poses
some major questions, even if it is to be funnelled through the all
embracing trust and participation cushion of the Cassells Committee approach.

It was conditions within generation which produced the first
human resource management initiative in the ESB in the late
1980s. As the inflexibilities within stations are maintained, such
as demarcations and the limits on the use of outside contractors, it
is clear the generation business will receive the greatest management attention and ultimately provide the greatest test of the new
strategy. Developments at Moneypoint, which will be examined in
the next chapter, bear testimony on this point. Generation is also
the side of the business where, in many cases, the management is
perceived to be weakest in terms of willingness and ultimate ability to adapt to the type of persuasion/participation/trust strategy
being promoted.

Distribution is seen as inherently more flexible and the area
where management is closer to its workforce and generally less
rule book- and agreement-orientated than station culture. Generation also faces a reduction in the numbers working having
largely escaped in the past, but this cannot occur unless the barrier to the use of outside contractors is lifted. The issue of flexibility and manning is inextricably linked in the power stations, according to one senior executive, who says that the numbers

employed within them should be lower.

The differing visions outlined by Cassells and McKinsey for the ESB passed one of their first tests with agreement on new manning levels for the first phase of the new Poolbeg 150 megawatt gas cycle station. In Corby in the UK, where the ESB manage a station, there are 40 staff for a station producing 400 megawatts. The corresponding Irish figure in a station of a similar size is about 120 staff.

The tradition of "tough" management, particularly in generation, who operated the "no give policy" in the past raises major questions as to their ability to lead a dualist strategy. Some senior management figures in the Board are wholly behind the twin track approach of Cassells and McKinsey as the only route to the future. Others see naked competition itself as the single most vital driver for change.

A major drag or inertia factor on the changes proposed is the highly integrated nature of the collective bargaining system operated in the ESB and the machinery and commercial monopoly which underpins it. This is best exemplified by the pay relationships between the staff categories and the tradition that an offer to one must spread to all. At a shopfloor level in the stations, where union resistance to management change operates across the stations rather than just within each one, this represents a major barrier to the 1994 CCR proposals. The introduction of local bargaining for each station, and the creation of a less confrontational environment to ease such change, thus represents a major challenge. One senior figure said that he saw line management in the stations having greater control in the future. In the longer term the unions will do less of their business centrally than at present. High levels of overtime, particularly in the stations, are also a restraining factor.

Political Intervention

Both Cassells and McKinsey are silent on the issue of political intervention in ESB, as is the bulk of the literature on the introduction of human resource management. The varying dimensions of political control in relation to the Board's prices, its investment decisions and wages, as well as the political exchange between the unions and Government at central and local level, are ignored. There is nothing in the recent history of the ESB that suggests these interventions, which have featured during pluralistic relations, are likely to cease or be lessened in the context of a human resource policy. In fact, if anything, the external changes in Government and official attitude forged by the dispute may increase the level of intervention. The introduction of a successful HRM policy, on the other hand, demands that the Government stand back and allow management and staff jointly shape their own futures.

Conclusion

The landscape of worker management relations in the ESB has been radically altered by the complex outcomes of the April 1991 electricians' dispute. While both the Cassells and McKinsey blueprints represent an internally-driven initiative at structured change, in both the IR and commercial fields, the ultimate accelerator of change will be the external environment in terms of competition and a more demanding shareholder — the Government — and the pressure of downsizing itself. The complex web of multi-layered bargaining — a "no risk" internal pay adjudication system and the sheer strength of union power, particularly in the stations — will mean that change will be slow and incremental. The Government is effectively using a price rise as a carrot to induce all in the ESB to accept the level of painful change, outlined in the Cost and Competitiveness Review. But the process is taking place against the background of the earlier Cassells Review which stresses partnership and trust, and which allowed both sides to take on new roles and partially wipe out the past.

The immediate aftershock of the dispute and a less benign political environment has already led to the union acceptance of the McKinsey plan to subdivide the Board into five divisions. Without the dispute, this might not have occurred without a battle. Channelling the level of structural change envisaged by management and by the CCR Review through the complicated and unwieldy Cassells process, and getting agreement, will be difficult. It will require a particularly sensitive as well as a consistent and coherent management strategy, especially within generation. Middle management attitudes have been seen in the past as the weak link in this process by many. But the opening of the process and the removal of explicit union marginalisation from the agenda has already created a positive mood and a good initial response.

A major difficulty will arise on the cross-over from a highly centralised system of bargaining to local arrangements, which will be based on local efficiencies, within stations and regions. Clearly the backlog of issues from the pluralist agenda presents a major problem. Wrapping up outstanding category negotiations in the context of an increasingly restrictive national pay policy, closely monitored by Government authorities, could prove difficult. Senior figures have said that they believe it unlikely that the level of structural change required, especially in stations, can be introduced without some industrial relations difficulties. The pitfalls in the new strategy are immense: the highly complex outcome of the dispute puts the major responsibility on management. Some of the difficulties associated with introducing a human resource strategy in one station, of the type considered by Cassells and McKinsey, are tentatively explored in the next chapter on developments in Moneypoint.

Chapter Eight

INTRODUCING CHANGE IN AN ADVERSARIAL ENVIRONMENT: THE MONEYPOINT EXPERIENCE

Background

By providing an outline of the difficulties associated with a human resource management style intervention in one major station, this chapter seeks to pinpoint examples of potential problem areas that may arise in the Board's wider HR change programme currently underway throughout the company. Human resource literature, while strong on the core values necessary to transform organisations at a macro level is notably weak on handling the cross-over from one system to the other at the level of the plant. While the Moneypoint intervention had different roots to the more planned change initiatives introduced in other stations, its development highlights the variety of factors, many of them highly localised, that can retard implementation elsewhere.

The ESB is critically dependent on the 900 megawatt Moneypoint power station, which supplies forty per cent of national output, making it extremely vulnerable to "instant disruptions". Against the background of a rash of unofficial strikes, the Board's Chief Executive launched a unique personal initiative. Different groups had stopped work on eight occasions over a nine month period, from December 1990 to September 1991, but most stoppages lasted less than half a day. Five further unofficial actions were launched in the six months after the letter. He wrote to each of the 415 workers in Moneypoint station individually expressing "deep concern" at the number of disputes which were leading to a disruption in operations and threatened supply to customers.

The Chief Executive told staff that he was arranging for an immediate "in-depth" study to be carried out over a four week period by an independent party and that this would provide "both sides with a basis to jointly tackle the problems". This intervention, which as we shall see later was to raise as many questions for local management as it did for staff unions, has to be seen in the wider context of the mood of crisis which still permeated the Board in the months after the nerve shattering April 1991 strike.

Moneypoint's Separate Change Process

The manner, style and reasoning behind the Chief Executive's intervention at Moneypoint was totally different from the change processes initiated in the other stations under the control of the Director of Generation, which had a company-wide focus and origin. The Moneypoint intervention resulted from a fear of the fall-out of further damaging strikes in the immediate aftermath of the April 1991 dispute. Questions were raised during the strike about the desirability of so much vital Generation capacity being controlled by one company in a single location at Moneypoint. The move by the Chief Executive was aimed at "keeping the lid" on Moneypoint during a particularly sensitive time and achieved some success. Issued after a series of unofficial actions, many of them related to an unpaid "station award", which had been a bone of contention since the late 1980s, the letter can be seen as the act of a management still caught up in the post strike trauma. The change processes in other stations had been introduced as part of the New Generation Programme, which was geared to boost performance and initially launched in late 1990.

The Chief Executive's initiative ran counter to the central recommendation of the Management of Change report: that the station manager should "personally lead and have responsibility for the change process in his own station." The Chief Executive's Moneypoint intervention, and the consultant that was brought in to drive the process were ultimately concerned with similar values to the broad human resource management programme in the rest of generation, including winning the commitment of staff, breaking down divisions between categories through the creation of cross functional teams and the building of trust. Separation of employee relations issues out of the industrial relations system was also paramount. But the timing of the intervention, at the peak of summer industrial unrest over a "station claim," served to complicate the process. It ultimately created unreal expectations that the initiative would produce short term palliatives and bring immediate and demonstrable results in terms of the ongoing IR agenda.

The strategic importance of Moneypoint, which employs 415, can be gauged from that the fact that its capacity is double that of the six peat stations in the Midland and West region which between them employ 1,000 people. Burning coal, it produces the cheapest electricity in the ESB system and has been subject to industrial unrest in recent years. The country's huge dependence on its output has meant that it is a major target for the unions contemplating system wide disruption or utilizing their raw muscle to curb supplies. Before looking at the station's change programme, it is worthwhile looking at some of the IR issues that later fed into the initiative, filtering its impact and confusing its role. The aim of the chapter is to highlight in a practical way the difficulties of achieving cultural and attitudinal change, with the long term goal of boosting performance, in a highly structured industrial relations environment.

Industrial Relations Background

Moneypoint generating station was commissioned gradually in the years 1985 to 1987. Salary scales applicable to the largest stations already in the system, Tarbert, Poolbeg and Aghada were applied. The issue of "imported" pay rates and the absence of a scale to reflect the size and the strategic role of the station has been a source of grievance up to the lodging of a twenty five per cent pay claim by all station staff, at first verbally, through their shop stewards in 1989. The station manager rejected the claim and asked for a written submission. After being rejected by local management, the claim lay dormant for fifteen months.

An internal management meeting held in Limerick in September 1989 between the Station Manager, the Director of Generation and other senior executives pin-pointed ten different causes of staff unrest in Moneypoint. These included the mix of staff from different working backgrounds and cultures; the drop in earnings compared with former jobs; social and domestic problems associated with the move to West Clare; disappointment that Moneypoint did not have enhanced rates and frustration at Board resistance to category claims and delays in processing claims generally.

In October 1990 the 25 per cent station claim was reactivated and the management said it did not feel any increase was justified. The immediate background to the claim was an eight per cent rise for productivity in the Marina station linked to the impact of gas, and settlements averaging four per cent in Moneypoint for supervisors and engineers.

The Board's Joint Industrial Council in a recommendation in May 1991 offered all staff an eight per cent rise as part of an overall Moneypoint Agreement, which was to subsume all existing agreements. Failure to agree on the balance of outstanding issues in the run up to the August 1991 deadline with key groups, led to the rise in unofficial action and the issuing of the Chief Executive's letter in September 1991. Management believes that key groups delayed the negotiations process because they wanted to get the full award, or the balance due to them, without making concessions.

Immediate Backdrop

Apart from lack of trust, the major stumbling block to the change process in Moneypoint was the continual spill over from the ongoing IR agenda within the station and the expectations raised by the timing of the intervention. The IR issues which impacted on the smooth starting of the initiative ranged from the withholding of a three per cent pay rise, part of the overall eight per cent station award, to the unusual issue of housing. Despite the fact that the station was completed in 1984, the housing issue was not finally resolved. Some staff from outside the area bought sites at inflated prices and later had difficulty paying for them, being lumbered with bridging finance as well as the difficulty of selling their old homes. An initial assistance scheme was later modified on an ad hoc basis and the fact that the overall programme was controlled outside the station resulted in delays and inconsistencies of treatment. The Board had provided an assistance package to married staff who transferred into the Moneypoint area in the form of subsidised mortgages, developed sites, bridging finance guarantees and advances of some interest payments. Staff were assisted in building 120 houses in West Clare at a substantial cost to the Board. Sites were bought at inflated prices locally and some Dublin staff sold their houses at near loss figures ahead of a property boom.

The problem with housing and the acknowledged mishandling of the assistance programme was only exacerbated by the failure of some staff from outside the region to settle in the West Clare area, which contributed to the unrest. Overtime was also being reduced: prior to 1987 it would have been over 50 or 60 per cent of earnings but it later fell to about 30 per cent. Failure to resolve the housing issue had resulted in it becoming a significant item on the station IR agenda, in the way that "everything in the ESB was IR".

Intervention

The manner and method of the intervention in Moneypoint was to present major difficulties for both sides, but particularly for management. A consultant in organisational behaviour was sent into Moneypoint by the Chief Executive of the ESB after he issued a letter to each member of staff in September 1991 following a volatile period of industrial unrest. Station executives believed there was a lack of clarity about the consultant's role and whether his reporting relationship was with local management, the Chief Executive or the Director of Generation. Local management were believed to have resented the style of the intervention.

Differences of opinion arose between the consultant and one of the station managers who wanted the more broadly based change management group, which was the vehicle used in other stations, to get involved. The manager was later promoted to another post within ESB Generation. A change in management, which resulted in the initiative becoming part of the wider change group within the company, later emerged.

A pre-intervention attitude survey carried out at Moneypoint revealed negative views about management/ staff relations, particularly in relation to the perceived lack of openness in communication. The strongest negative feelings were found among supervisors. The first element of the consultant's three stage intervention in Moneypoint was the gathering of information from management and staff aimed at identifying the concerns of all on the isolated County Clare site. Strong negative attitudes towards management/staff relations emerged in line with the findings of the 1990 survey and the information was then presented back to the key groups. The response of local management to the data was that it was not factual (McCabe, 1993: 25). The management feeling was that the findings were inadequate and one sided, but not biased towards any particular group or one point of view.

A Participation Council has been in existence in Moneypoint since 1985. Its main areas of involvement were staff newsletters and putting foward proposals on such issues as long service awards and sick leave draws. One option considered by management was that the Council should act as the Steering Group in tackling the issues that had been thrown up as a result of the fact finding exercise. The shop stewards group in the station had historically "held onto" the major issues. When any major issue was being diverted into the Council that posed a threat to their own

position they opposed it. But difficulties arose over the representation of staff:

> It became apparent that other groupings such as shop stewards
> saw themselves as representing staff. Attempts at reconciling
> the various interested parties at this stage proved unsuccessful
> (McCabe,1993: 33).

The shop stewards in the station did not trust the Participation
Council. The unions had tended not to put their most able people
onto it, simply because they saw it as a threat to the role and
strength of existing shop stewards system. The shop stewards
would have liked to have divested themselves of a lot of their
agenda that was not industrial relations. But they were afraid
that they could lose their total hold on IR, if they let too many
other issues slip into other areas, such as the Participation
Council. The shop stewards did not want to reject the initiative
because they felt it would have been "thrown back" into their
faces. They believed that management would simply have said "we
offered you this solution as a way out but you rejected it". Being
reluctant participants, they did not see the consultant as
"roughing up any of management's feathers" and felt that in the
early phases of the initiative, in the information gathering phase,
he was having too many meetings with management.

The view was that the initiative within the Board was so big
that it contained within it "lethal" potential for doing away with
the normal IR channels which were recognised as "not being per-
fect". As the union representative put it: "If you gave management
too much of a lead they would not be too long about galloping on".

The internal politics of the station, particularly the balance of
power between the Participation Council and the formal union arrangements created difficulties in setting up a transitional structure to mediate and oversee the change process. McCabe (1993:
34) identifies four key players in the entire process: local senior
management; middle managers and supervisors; the Participation
Council and the Shop Stewards' Committee. Despite efforts to create "a collaborative" framework, various groups saw themselves
losing out.

Local management favoured the Participation Council as the
vehicle for change and identified issues for consideration including
mechanisms for staff input to business plans, opportunities for
personal development of staff, and identification with the Moneypoint station. To surmount the problem of using the Participation

Council as a Steering Committee, meetings were held with all the groups involved, the Council itself, middle managers and supervisors, shop stewards and senior management. Further "in depth" meetings similar to the management workshops were held for the key three groups, senior managers, middle managers and shop stewards, with the aspiration of creating a cross-functional group. This larger grouping consisted of 36 people. The middle management/supervisory group made the point that all staff should be informed of events and they warned of high levels of resistance or mistrust. About 60 people were involved in the whole process and emphasis was placed on probing the desired future state envisaged by the groups. A large measure of agreement was found on the issues affecting the station. The plan was to hold one joint meeting of all three groups to consider tackling issues together. Shop stewards representing the electricians failed to attend after management withdrew three per cent of the eight per cent station award for participating in a work to rule in December 1992. The electricians, an influential group, had taken their action in support of colleagues in nearby Tarbert station. The unions argued that the action had been "imported" from another station but the management believed that it was ruled out of bounds by the nature of the peace clause and withdrew the three per cent. As McCabe (1993: 55) puts it:

> Although all agreed that the involvement approach was the right way to go, the adversarial environment was a trap into in which it was not difficult to succumb (sic).

The major issues that the shop stewards fed into the debate were the housing issue, the question of a special rate for Moneypoint, the lack of trust within the station and inter category issues. When the shop stewards moved into the bigger nine person group, later known as the Communications Review Group, with the management and the Participation Council, they felt that the ground had changed considerably and that their own problems were being sidelined.

The unions had believed that the initiative would have cleared up some of the outstanding issues, particularly the question of the Moneypoint rate. The fact that the Chief Executive's initiative was launched in September 1991, in the wake of a series of unofficial actions and when the station rate issue was not totally resolved, only contributed to this belief in the eyes of the union official:

> We felt that if the consultant could have organised that man-
> agement addressed the problem of a Moneypoint rate, and
> could have got it over with, instead of it dragging on we could
> have got somewhere. But we never got a chance to voice the
> station rate. We were waiting for this huge report and recom-
> mendations which never appeared.

One early proposal to create a huge poster within the station with
the picture and location telephone number of each member of staff
on it ran into some difficulty. This was aimed at breaking down
the anonymity within the station. Getting the project off the
ground would have had a symbolic value. But some members of
staff have said that they do not want their photograph to be used.

The unions perceived the outside consultant to have widened
his brief at a certain point, which later made them reluctant to
have him participate in the continuing process:

> The way management talks it is out to reduce the number of
> people working in Moneypoint. The consultant tried to keep it
> separate in the beginning. He correlated common ground. You
> realize the same things are appearing all the time. But he went
> from nitty gritty points that were irking people in Moneypoint
> to change management. At a certain point he moved onto the
> management's agenda of the change process.

Station management had been drawing up plans for the next five
years and presented these to the Participation Council. They
looked at issues like staff reductions, reduced overtime, structural
changes and competition. This however caused annoyance among
the shop stewards who regarded the management as presenting
their plans to the wrong forum.

But there is a great reluctance among the unions to give the
outside consultant a continuing role in Moneypoint at the time of
writing for a number of reasons:

> He tends to take control. He knows the game. He has too much
> influence and if he makes a suggestion we must follow it. We
> are more independent when he is not there. We can try and ne-
> gotiate on our own agenda.

Management for their part recognize what they see as a marked
reticence to the consultant being brought in again:

> It is clear that the unions are more comfortable working locally.
> It is a difficulty for management and for the Board at the mo-
> ment.

McCabe stresses (1993: 57) that the intervention in Moneypoint to date has shown "how complicated such a process can be to get off the ground". He is convinced that a full time facilitator is needed in the station to advance the initiative. While many of the substantive issues raised are capable of being solved locally others are beyond the scope of the process, such as autonomy and changing the reward system. Underlying many of the attitudes in Moneypoint was what has been described as the "superstation mentality", based on the station's flagship status within the grid and the sheer national dependency on its output. As one executive explained it:

> They see themselves as the superstation. But if they go the full way they will want a share of the rewards. The thinking in management is also altering to saying we should get rid of centralised negotiations and let each station make their own deal according to their own conditions.

All of the foregoing suggests a slow and highly gradual process to the building of cultural change in a station environment. While management originally saw the consultant's role in terms of "climate assessment" the unions saw him in essentially an ombudsman role, ironing out difficulties like an honest broker. However the industrial relations issues kept filtering through into the initiative and posing a threat to it. Ultimately the major debates and rows were over process and not really about substantive issues. When a real issue emerged that both sides agreed was relevant to the Communications Steering Group, there was no difficulty agreeing a modus operandi for furthering it. Management's perception of the whole process, as an initiative aimed at improving performance in the longer term and its "hard" aspirations for its outcome, are totally different to union expectations, which are essentially focussed on improving communications. This hard and soft emphasis between the parties on the one initiative mirrors macro developments within the ESB.

The Micro Dynamics of Change — The Moneypoint Experience

The Moneypoint initiative represents a pragmatic response to a mounting problem of unofficial action which was ultimately shaped by human resource management values. The Chief Executive's initial approach and agenda found little favour with local line management, largely because of the way it was imposed, following a crisis. HRM theory (Beer and Spector, 1985; and Storey, 1992) all highlight the importance of shared management goals on issues that affect the relationships between the organisation and its employees as a prerequisite to any initiative aimed at eliciting commitment. Developments at Moneypoint suggest that backing from the Chief Executive alone will not guarantee success and the importance of line management being involved from the initial, design and formulation of the process, not just its implementation. Management consensus was initially absent. The Chief Executive's intervention in the middle of a series of unofficial industrial actions contradicted the central principle of the Board's own change programme for stations and one of the core propositions of the theory of human resource management: that line managers drive the entire change/participation/ trust process. The evidence from Moneypoint pinpoints the major pitfalls in launching a human resource type initiative in an environment with a deeply embedded adversarial industrial relations system and culture. Aside from the bargaining issues of pay and job security, particular local conditions such as difficulties over housing and unease with social arrangements, served to reinforce traditional suspicions of new forms of organisation and management. The limited research carried out on developments in Moneypoint for this book, which should be treated cautiously, suggests four different lines of internal conflict associated with the intervention itself, which impaired the introduction of HRM values at the station.

Firstly, through by-passing local management and the Directorate responsible for Generation, the Chief Executive undermined one of the core principles of the change programme, which were in embryonic form in September 1991. In the process he undermined his own management.

Secondly, the internal distrust within the unions of their own colleagues on the Participation Council and their fear of "croneyism" within it, acted as a brake and resulted in the people with IR dominance holding sway. This meant that when the steering forum for the initiative, the Communications Review Group, was eventually set up, people with the strongest IR experience could exert control.

Thirdly, the "dualistic" tensions between both pillars of the initiative, the industrial relations arm and efforts at opening communications/trust/participation threw up several neutralizing factors. Staff were simultaneously being asked to share a future agenda with management for station co-operation while at the same time face reductions in numbers, cutbacks in overtime and an era of almost constant change through benchmarking with similar operations elsewhere.

Finally, aside from the initiative itself, straightforward collective bargaining problems were being handled locally and centrally and produced their own difficulties. A proposal to convert Moneypoint to run on oil as well as coal, for reasons of security of supply, was rejected by the unions who wanted a five per cent payment and a £1,000 lump sum. This claim was processed by the Joint Industrial Council centrally and turned down.

All of these conflicts have to be seen within the overall context of management's "dualist strategy" and the separating out of industrial relations from broader relations built on trust, openness and commitment to change. Inevitably the issues raised in the IR channel will pose major difficulties to improving relations through alternative communications, at a time of rapid change and pressure on prices and numbers.

Conclusion

Developments at the Moneypoint demonstrate the fragility of the change process, particularly in the context of a "dualist approach" and the continuing overspill from the IR agenda. At a management level, experience in the station suggests that Chief Executive support alone will not guarantee success, but that wider line management backing is vital. The lesson of Moneypoint is that accumulated distrust and in particular local circumstances can provide major obstacles to progress. The creation of new forums to promote more harmonious relationships open up new opportunities for station politics and adds a further layer of complexity.

However it has to be said that whatever about the local difficulties, the chief executive's intervention resulted in a lowering of the temperature in Moneypoint at a particularly crucial and sensitive time for the Board. In retrospect it resulted in sidelining of particularly difficult issues until plans of greater momentum and importance, McKinsey's 1994 proposals for the entire Board, were to surface for all staff with huge implications for the type of issues raised in Moneypoint. Half of the 412 jobs at the station are scheduled to go under the plan.

Chapter Nine

CONCLUSIONS

Introduction

The past year, 1994, looks set to go down in recent history as a watershed year for Irish semi-state companies for a number of reasons. The question of their ownership, control and structure provoked a major debate, particularly in relation to the future of Telecom Éireann, one of the largest companies in the State sector employing over 13,000 people. And the Government's stake in a number of financial institutions is the subject of serious private sector interest, which may see a partial or total sell-off, depending on the outcome of various negotiations. In parallel, the numbers employed in semi-state firms continues to decline: the total number of employees in key commercial semi-states has dropped by five per cent since 1990. (See Appendix I).

But most of all, it was industrial relations issues — particularly the summer-long disputes at TEAM Aer Lingus and Irish Steel, and the unprecedented level of change tabled in the autumn in the ESB, through demands for 2,900 job cuts — which provoked the most debate and attracted most attention to the semi-state companies. Much of this debate centred on the public perception that the most difficult and intractable disputes were breaking out in the state sector, while the private sector had managed to reach settlements peacefully. The public also found it difficult to fathom why people in relatively secure state-backed employment, much of it craft-based, found it so difficult to change in order to survive.

Remarkably, the type of restructuring disputes, which both TEAM and Irish Steel represent, and both of which led to a serious questioning of the roles of management and unions in these companies, do not even figure in traditional industrial dispute statistics. Days lost nationally due to strikes in the first nine months of 1994 were the lowest on record at 18,522 (Quinn, 1994) but over 100,000 days were lost in the high-profile rows in TEAM and Irish Steel. But because no formal strike notice was served in either case, with lay-offs over cost-cutting at the heart of both rows, the huge days-lost total does not come within the ambit of the traditional index of industrial unrest. This just underscores how unconventional the disputes at Irish Steel and TEAM actually were. If the 1980s was the decade of retrenchment on job numbers in semi-states, when total employment was cut by 24 per cent over 10 years (Sweeney, 1991), the 1990s looks set to go down as an era of more fundamental change, when traditional workplace patterns and collective bargaining arrangements themselves came under threat from a variety of new more commercial pressures.

The dominance of the post-war model of industrial relations, based on adversarial collective bargaining and joint rule setting, may not endure in its current form in the longer term in these new conditions. Before teasing out the implications of both rows, and of other recent high profile semi-states disputes, including the developments in the ESB, a short review of the forces shaping change will be considered.

The New Change Agenda

Chapter One examined the way in which Irish semi-state companies are facing new and uncontrollable pressures on a number of fronts which are in the main external. These forces roughly fall under three headings: demands for greater commercialisation from Government, European deregulation and the management requirement to cut costs and introduce new work practices.

This new agenda was given concrete expression by two recent Government reports which underline the changed approach to state companies: the Culliton Report (*Report of the Industrial Policy Review Group*, January 1992) and the Moriarty Report (*Employment Through Enterprise — the Response of the Government to the Moriarty Task Force Report on the Implementation of the Culliton Report*, May 1993). These reports' major concern is with the prices charged and services provided to the wider economy by the semi-states and the importance of injecting a market responsiveness into their operations.

Traditional management approaches, which emphasise accountability above all, are being questioned and a new generation of chief executives, who have no background in the State sector, is being recruited to adopt a firmer and tougher approach to the companies under their control. This new approach often involves facing down traditional union power, and the embedded practices it seeks to protect.

The disputes in TEAM, Irish Steel, Aer Lingus, Irish Rail and earlier rows in An Post and RTE highlight the difficulty of introducing change into working environments which were up to recently shielded from these harsher commercial pressures. By late 1994, the Irish semi-state sector is facing into the sort of change and rationalisation programmes that were the hallmark of many serious private sector disputes in the 1980s. But not all semi-state companies have been through a crisis; the key question of why some can handle change and others cannot will be addressed later.

The traditional pluralist systems of industrial relations that operate in these firms have had major difficulty coming to terms with the demands of the new agenda, which include pay cuts, demands for the introduction of contract workers and numerical and work flexibility. The inability of the formalised negotiating procedures to handle the level of change demanded had led to a crisis in many of these companies, most recently TEAM and Irish Steel, where initiatives on behalf of several dispute resolving agencies failed to find a settlement. TEAM had to go into interim examinership before the crucial crafts worker group accepted the need for work practice and pay changes and dramatically reversed their earlier rejection of Labour Court proposals. Irish Steel was teetering on the brink of liquidation when the craft group at its Cobh plant finally accepted the rescue plan.

The unprecedented level of demands tabled in these firms represents a major challenge to the pluralist orthodoxy of joint rule-setting and dispute resolution which has dominated the practice of industrial relations in Ireland, and semi-state companies in particular, for the last three decades. Taken in total, the new demands, fuelled by increasing global competition and deregulation, represent the rising dominance of an employer-led agenda in Irish industrial relations. This has major implications not only for the role of trade unions generally, but particularly for how they are to respond to such changes in the longer term and publicly avoid appearing to adopt a totally defensive strategy.

The unyielding demands for major change, now appearing to surface in semi-state companies, imply a much altered relationship between semi-state companies and Government. The role of Government as shareholder is itself undergoing a fundamental shift with an increasing reluctance to cushion State firms from major change on the basis of some of their former social functions.

The Government mandate to semi-state companies is that they become fully commercialised, responsive to market needs and sensitive to the prices they charge.

This more demanding Government mandate also has major implications for the traditional relationships between unions and politicians in the overall semi-state context. The tripartite model of political exchange between Government, management and unions, under which the latter group saw those in political power as having ultimate control, and as such being part of any settlement, is undergoing modification. Recent events suggest that the Government wants to scale down its role as a player in semi-state industrial relations and particularly its function as a last port of call in a crisis. But the ownership issue will mean that the Government can never quite remove itself from the stage altogether. In future, it may want to confine its role to setting the parameters of policy, but the temptation and pressure to stray into operational areas, is likely to remain in the Irish political context of proportional representation. Developments in the summer of 1994 in both TEAM and Irish Steel, suggest that increasingly ministers are willing to adopt a more hands-off approach when faced with intense political pressure and major industrial relations trauma. But any change in this approach is likely to be a slow and gradual process. The sensitive political nature of many of the services provided by the semi-state companies suggests that any possible convergence between public and private sector styles of industrial relations, as speculated on by some writers, will ultimately be limited. The adoption of private sector management models by the semi-state sector alone will not bridge the gap.

Disputes considered in Chapter One highlight the emerging challenges to the pluralist orthodoxy of traditional industrial relations in terms of numerical flexibility, work practice changes and alterations to shift and work patterns. The strongest and most developed line of challenge to the conventional model of industrial relations bargaining has emerged within ESB, particularly since the 1991 dispute, which proved to be a major catalyst for change and external examination, particularly on costs.

The issue at the centre of the 1991 dispute, which saw slightly over 7,000 ESB workers strike causing widespread disruption to industry, was an electricians' five per cent pay claim. Formal rejection by the Board's 24-year-old internal industrial relations machinery, the Joint Industrial Council (JIC), led to the TEEU serving strike notice. The Personnel Directorate failed to anticipate the strike would take place immediately. As a result, the country lurched unprepared into industrial and social chaos, with up to 10,000 workers laid off at a cost of tens of millions of pounds to the economy. While only 100 of the striking electricians worked in generation, support from other groups, including shift workers, ensured its effectiveness. This support was linked to the "unfinished business" the various groups had with management rather than the merits of the electricians' own claim. The initial response from management was to treat the strike sanction from the TEEU as just another threat of industrial action. The approach operated by management was consistent with their handling of other disputes: allow it go through procedures, accept the outcome and then stand by it.

The major contributory factors to the 1991 dispute were thus perceived to be a threat to the Joint Industrial Council process; an offer of a £10,000 lump sum and five per cent to fitters for allowing outside contractors into generating stations and an overhang of frustration from the tough management stance taken during the 1980s best summed up in the "no give policy". The four day strike of April 1991 unleashed a level of public criticism of the ESB and its senior executives of a type never experienced by the Board.

The most significant immediate outcome of the strike was that it seriously undermined the role of industrial relations in the Board, and any residual belief that, along with existing personnel policy, it could deliver the level of change needed for the future. This crisis of collective bargaining provided an opening for the alternative human resource strategy which had been in train in generation since 1988, on the side of the business facing competition from European deregulation. The dispute also led to a Joint Management/Union Review of Relationships (The Cassells Report), which was heavily influenced by "soft" human resource concepts of trust and participation, partly based on the initiative launched in generation. Coupled with the later McKinsey Report into the structures of the ESB, the two studies have provided a new agenda for the current level of change being sought.

However, contradictions exist within and between these initiatives. Cassells proposes the maintenance of adversarial collective bargaining alongside the development of trust and participation. McKinsey vests much more control in management than Cassells, calls for a "bias for action" and proposes a "harder" and more performance-focused version of HRM than Cassells. But the price of accepting Cassells — with its aspirations to "soft" HRM — and ultimately the McKinsey plan for the break up into five separate business units is the maintenance of the existing collective bargaining structure and the centralised pay machinery.

Like the creation of the Cassells Committee before it, the agreement by ESB management and unions to carry out an internal review of costs in February 1994, in response to a earlier review announced by the Government in November 1993, can be seen as defensive strategy. The Department of Transport, Energy and Communications eventually agreed to become part of the Cost and Competitiveness Review (CCR) of ESB, launched by the management and unions in the company. This review eventually led to the new set of McKinsey proposals, including 2,900 job losses, which were published in Autumn of 1994 and are now the subject of negotiation.

This package, produced in response to ministerial reluctance to grant the first price increase since 1986, represents one of the broadest and most thorough agendas for change ever tabled in a semi-state company. The range of both organisational and work practice changes being sought represent one of the strongest challenges yet posed to the dominance of the post-war model of pluralist industrial relations in a semi-state company.

The demands are based on studies of best international practice in other utilities, in which the unions participated, and as such are not found in any one operation. In generation, numbers would be halved under the proposals, management de-layered from the current six levels and overtime cut from an average of 18 per cent to eight. The key to the changes will be the unlocking of existing agreements, particularly those which guarantee overtime, the use of outside contractors and new work practices. The range of changes sought by McKinsey, including cutting payments above basic pay; removing demarcations, reducing manning on overhauls; operational staff "stepping up and stepping down" on jobs; and a four day working week of 10 hours per day in transmission and distribution.

Crisis-Driven or Planned Change

The latest McKinsey proposals for ESB represent a planned and managed change process in the wake of the crisis of industrial relations in the Board produced by the 1991 dispute. Looking back on the 1991 strike recently and the follow-on impact to all sides in the ESB, one senior and well placed figure noted: "If there had not been a 1991 strike, we would have had to invent one". His essential point was that the strike was a catalyst; that a set of conditions existed in the Board prior to 1991 that were literally waiting for someone to put a spark to set them alight. The other implication is that without the 1991 dispute and the shock it delivered to both sides in the ESB, the level of change necessary within the Board would not have been achieved. The strike did emerge, and in time it altered both the internal and external ground rules faced by the company in a way that is not yet complete. At the time of writing, the ESB is literally in a state of transformation with the post-strike Cassells Committee initiative having given both sides a way of distancing themselves from their former entrenched positions. With the crisis in the company now well past, the major question to be asked of the current process is how changed will the ESB be that emerges from the talks on the McKinsey plan.

Developments within the semi-state sector generally, and the ESB in particular, raise questions as to whether a crisis, internally or externally generated, is necessary to introduce change, particularly in the industrial relations arena. Some Irish personnel executives, including some in the ESB, are known to support the "big bang" approach, basically taking the view that they can introduce and implement more of their agenda when everything is on the table in a fully blown strike or dispute situation. The heretofore quite restrictive bargaining culture within the semi-states may have produced a climate where this approach was seen as a viable and attractive option. Others put more refined language on the same position and suggest that a series of "climactic shocks" are necessary to induce ongoing acceptance of change. Industrial relations theory, on the other hand, suggests that a compromise exists for every problem and that a resolution can be found which will maintain the existing framework of workplace relations intact. Much of human resource management thinking "builds-in" a constant change process in the sort of workplace models it seeks to introduce.

One key issue is whether the dynamism and momentum introduced by a crisis can be sustained in more orderly every day conditions, or whether the organisation will retreat back into the approach which resulted in the crisis in the first place. The role and quality of management in the new situation is crucial here and whether it can be seen to have learnt the lessons of the past in terms of its former approach. This question automatically leads on to the issue of why some organisations can achieve change without a crisis and what particular conditions produce a climate within which change can be peacefully accommodated. During the TEAM crisis, for example, another Aer Lingus subsidiary, Airmotive, which also operates in an aviation-related business, signed with little difficulty a significant agreement with its unions, many of them crafts unions, on pay and rationalisation. The Airmotive plant is located in West Dublin, well away from the Dublin Airport complex and was not surrounded by the political controversy which marked TEAM's inception or its later efforts at restructuring. Some of the recent success stories of semi-state change have occurred in companies like Bord na Móna, Bord Gáis and ACC Bank, which like Airmotive were not high profile operations. Location, company culture and the history of bargaining relations may therefore be influences which bear down on the acceptability or otherwise of change along with a range of other factors, some of them difficult to define.

Many involved in introducing the Cahill plan in Aer Lingus believe that it was the conditioning created by the previous plan in 1990 that ultimately laid the ground for the acceptability of what was to emerge in the final package. But other issues, like the quality of the union leadership and the highly competitive market realities faced by the airline's workforce on a daily basis, also played a part and set the Aer Lingus experience apart from what was to finally emerge within TEAM.

The key to the acceptance of change appears to be some level of planning and a conditioning process which makes staff aware of the external difficulties faced by their firm. This approach, however, demands a strong commitment to the creation of a communication process that goes beyond the traditional agendas of pay and conditions and which Irish managers have often been slow to embrace in deed, but not in word. Some trade unionists link resistance to change to the very nature of adversarial industrial relations itself. They stress the need for a change of attitude and approach on the part of those in control of firms aimed at fostering relations based on trust and breaking down suspicion.

But much management thinking tends to be based on the "if its not broken why fix it approach" and the sort of heavy accountability culture which exists within the public sector creates — some might say institutionalises — a caution which sustains this outlook. The traditional union response of leading from behind, which featured in some of the disputes but by no means all, tends to rest comfortably alongside this style of management. One leading trade union figure, with broad experience of the semi-state area, describes the overall quality of management in the sector with a few notable exceptions as "abysmal". Some external consultants who have done work in a number of State firms also comment critically on the quality of management and reiterate the view, commonly held, that too much of management thinking is internally directed, lacks a commercial focus and that more "outsiders" are needed. With the exception of a number of recent appointments to chief executive positions, management vacancies in semi-state companies are generally filled internally, which further heightens the overall internalisation process which features both in industrial relations and other decision making areas.

Another feature of the change programmes addressed in this chapter can be the lack of a real commitment on the part of management to what they are putting forward or proposing. Often middle management, who themselves are likely to be the first victims of change, are privately resistant to what is proposed and this may be communicated to the shopfloor. As one senior figure noted, confusion can result from the gap between what is said across the table at formal negotiating sessions and what is said privately within the plant.

But there are some indications that a new type of trade unionism is emerging in Ireland that demands a more strategic approach at a management level and will in turn deliver a more enlightened response to executives who are willing to lead with a more open style. But, as in the more traditional mode, strong trade unions demand strong management and vice versa. For example, there is some evidence that the country's largest union, SIPTU, is putting some of the lessons learnt in the Aer Lingus and Irish Steel experiences to use elsewhere, in terms of a model approach within which the union would play a more proactive role. The function of the union in this context goes beyond purely bargaining issues and it becomes a grouping which forces the pace on change, rather than merely adapting to it. But not all trade union officials or shop stewards are capable of driving the union role in this direction. And this is a problem which the leadership of the Irish Congress of Trades Unions and others are beginning to address both in terms of recruitment and training.

Organisationally, the sort of changes proposed at the ESB and some of the other semi-state companies will have major implications for unions in terms of the introduction of local bargaining and the introduction of pay flexibility. The creation of business units within the ESB could ultimately result in different pay structures being sought that would match the business and work conditions of the particular businesses. The introduction of performance-based pay at local levels with each station would see pay becoming much more of a lever of local management than it has been up to now. Pay would in effect be used as a tool of local managerial flexibility and be linked to the demands and changes sought, not only within each individual business unit, but under McKinsey within each individual generating station. In this scenario, the power and role of unions centrally would be much reduced. An across the board pay structure could still be negotiated centrally, but overall union power could be diluted if workers had significant elements of their pay set locally. The incentive for workers in one station to take action in support of workers in another station over pay would be significantly reduced in this situation. Each station could become a stand-alone pay unit. National industrial actions could be more difficult to organise under this sort of decentralisation. A less restrictive national pay policy may be required to accommodate these new types of pay systems.

One other significant aspect of many of the disputes considered here, including the ESB, was the role of the Irish Congress of Trades Unions in finding a resolution, and the use of several different dispute resolving agencies to find an eventual settlement. As discussed in Chapter One, TEAM and Irish Steel, because of their unique histories and the particular role played by crafts unions, were never going to be easy rows to solve. In its interventions the ICTU is acting both as a social partner and as the trade union umbrella body working for the better interest of the wider trade union movement by trying to head-off or resolve unseemly rows that bring unions into disrepute. While some senior figures see the role of the ICTU — which entered both rows after the Labour Relations Commission and Labour Court processes — as bringing the role of both institutions into disrepute and creating another informal loop in the process, it is too early to be definitive.

The Shape of the Future

The background to the crisis of pluralism in the ESB was the emergence of a "no risk" negotiating culture in which the process of the Joint Industrial Council dominated the issues. Management's tradition of accepting every Council recommendation, and the huge dependency on the Council to produce settlements to the major issues, led to it superseding and largely replacing the normal negotiating channels. Automatic acceptance of every decision created a range of expectations and a flood of claims which produced an overall imbalance in the system. It meant that the JIC system itself became the dominant feature of collective bargaining rather than operating as a Court of last resort when negotiations at local level became blocked. But suggestions for a two-tier JIC have been mooted that would allow for a conciliation process. Having failed to achieve reform of the Joint Industrial Council process through agreement with the unions, management responded by "toughening up" its own response to claims outside the council by adopting a more hard-line approach. This in turn only served to re-inforce the entire JIC process. Management's ability to seek reform of the JIC was not just circumscribed by union opposition but by Government unwillingness to confront the issue. As a result, opportunities for changing the industrial relations system were limited.

The crisis in ESB industrial relations provoked by the 1991 dispute was internally generated but acted as a catalyst for much greater external change, much of it market-driven, which is now to be implemented. The level of change being sought in the ESB is more far-reaching and has more implications for the practice of pluralist industrial relations than what has emerged elsewhere. As many academic writers have noted, the paradox of industrial relations is that it is being refashioned out of initiatives which have nothing to do with the reforms proposed by Lord Donovan in his seminal Royal Commission Report in 1968. Rather, its re-working, as has been recognised by both the Irish Congress of Trades Unions and Irish personnel executives, has arisen from external commercially driven forces which result in organisational restructuring, new operational methods and new and more flexible forms of working.

The existing category culture within the ESB, where separate pay arrangements are made with each group, will prove a major obstacle to management demands for demarcation and the introduction of new flexibilities, particularly in generation but also in distribution. Proposals for multi-skilling pose a major threat to the traditional status of craft unions. But the pooling or sharing of duties in stations, with operations staff required to do maintenance and craftsmen doing their own cleaning, will also have major implications for the number of general workers that will be needed in future. In addition, the inter-union factor cannot be ignored; some unions are more responsive to the management's new

McKinsey agenda than others and this could cause some difficulties in the negotiation process. The absence of final agreement at European level on the draft directives for the electricity industry open up a further bargaining space between the unions, the management and the Government. All these factors make getting final agreement on the latest McKinsey proposal a highly complex and difficult process. Some unions will also see a trade-off between the level of change being demanded and the level of price increase ultimately sanctioned by Government. As referred to earlier in the context of change generally, maintaining management support, particularly the commitment of middle and senior management, will be vital throughout the whole process. It is too early to predict the future role of existing ESB bargaining structures in the new regime currently under negotiation. Will they become a "safety net" to handle difficulties in the new bargaining relationship or simply wither away? Bodies like the JIC are more than likely to stay intact but may undergo reform.

Drawing on developments in both the ESB and the other semi-state companies, a number of observations can be made. First, pluralist industrial relations probably functions best under competitive external pressures, which up to recently were lacking in the ESB — an element of risk is necessary for both sides. Second, the global forces now bearing down on the operations of semi-state companies require planned change programmes rather than a crisis management response, which may have no lasting impact. Potential difficulties ahead need to be planned for with staff appraised of the downside as well as the upside to expansion and growth. Third, some semi-state management is very internally focused; greater use of outside appointments needs be made at all levels and not just the highest levels. Fourth, greater Government clarity about the role and function of semi-state companies is needed to avoid demands for political intervention dominating disputes. Fifth, a more proactive and strategic approach from unions, particularly crafts unions, is required if semi-state businesses are to be transformed to survive and perform in the new environment.

But where does all the talk and demand for change leave the unions, in terms of their role in the traditional bargaining hierarchy? Unions are conscious that in order to retain their relevance they need to give up some of their bargaining agenda, particularly in the area of flexibility. In order to maintain their power, they have to share it in the new situation. The fact that existing centralised bargaining arrangements, like those underpinning the PCW, afford them considerable influence at Governmental level allows for some risk-taking locally in response to genuine participative and open management initiatives. But unions face a fundamental dilemma in relation to the new forms of work organisation agenda. If they resist they face margainalisation and public attack, while moving onto management's agenda risks accusations that they are abandoning the traditional core values of unionism.

Finally, many recent writers on the subject of change have highlighted just how few managements and unions in workplaces have fully embraced the new forms of work organisation agenda. Managers and union leaders advocating innovative human resource practices have become "islands of innovation in a sea of traditional practices", one noted American academic wrote recently. Only time will tell whether the ESB and the other semi-state companies considered here will lead or lag in this respect.

APPENDIX I: EMPLOYMENT IN IRELAND'S MAJOR COMMERCIAL SEMI-STATE COMPANIES

Company	1980	1981	1982	1983	1984	1985	1986	1987	1988	1989	1990	1993	Change 1990/1993	
Aer Lingus (2)			5543	5193	5116	5060	4982	4844	4781	5108	5511	3571	-1940	-35.2%
A.C.C.	659	674	657	600	555	510	472	415	403	407	423	500	77	18.2%
Aer Rianta (3)	1958	1924	1869	1723	1703	1719	1718	1670	1667	1787	2041	2600	559	27.4%
Arramara	36	33	29	29	29	25	24	25	25	25	25	25	0	0.0%
B.G.E.	56	79	99	118	121	221	242	454	947	912	900	795	-105	-11.7%
Bord Na Móna	5998	6234	6071	5937	5694	5136	4687	4795	3835	3152	2673	2270	-403	-15.1%
Ceimicí Teo	143	140	134	126	67									
C.I.E.	16463	16211	15927	15374	14928	14295	13540	12906	11249	11078	10768	10289	-479	-4.4%
Coillte	3700	3530	3360	3190	3020	2850	2700	2600	2510	2041	1996	1597	-399	-20.0%
E.S.B.	12441	13301	13215	12792	12454	12114	11763	11383	10903	10724	10500	10028	-472	-4.5%
I.C.C.	253	325	379	390	363	336	319	322	350	361	355	303	-52	-14.6%
I.N.P.C.	16	16	16	169	169	154	155	181	180	179	192	222	30	15.6%
Irish Shipping	968	986	915	863	700									
Irish Steel	733	732	628	630	632	637	521	522	553	629	633	551	-82	-13.0%
N.E.T.	1498	1161	985	942	821	735	656	636	915	789	757	713	-44	-5.8%
R.T.E.	2367	2338	2302	2246	2376	2367	2333	2258	2146	2101	2010	1976	-34	-1.7%
Telecom Éireann	26255	26200	26201	18260	17260	15850	15080	14560	14270	13900	13552	13069	-483	-3.6%
An Post (4)				8900	8871	8948	8951	8392	7931	7865	7840	8532	692	8.8%
V.H.I.	246	282	270	278	276	276	282	289	328	388	362	379	17	4.7%
TOTALS	73790	74166	78600	77760	75155	71233	68425	66252	62993	61446	60538	57420	-3118	-5.2%
Privatised Companies														
B&I	2066	2050	1879	1747	1795	1829	1492	1411	945	897	850			
Irish	3558	3343	3145	2803	2596	2522	2205	1855	1687	1556	1757	1928	171	9.7%
Sugar/Greencore														
Irish Life	1288	1363	1400	1424	1480	1552	1635	1699	1853	1914	2036	2149	113	5.6%

Sources: Annual Reports of State Sponsored Bodies, also with assistance from some Companies. Sweeney (1991).

Notes: Figures from annual reports for year closest to calander year. Most figures are for end of year employment.
(2) Aer Lingus figures for Ireland only, excluding subsidiaries. (3) Aer Rianta figures include Dublin, Shannon and Cork, Aer Rianta International and G.S.H. taken over in 1990. (4) An Post — the bulk of the increase of 8.8% was accounted for by part-time and temporary staff.

APPENDIX II — RESEARCH METHODS

The research work for this book was carried out in two distinct and separate phases. Material for the first two chapters was gathered in late summer 1994 at the height of the Irish Steel and TEAM Aer Lingus disputes. The bulk of the research for the remainder of the book on the ESB was carried out in 1993 as part of the work for an M.COMM thesis at the Graduate School of Business in UCD.

The discussion and analysis in the first third of the book on the most recent crisis in the semi-states, is based on information, reports and documentation, the bulk of which is in the public domain, gathered by the author in his role as Industrial Correspondent with Independent Newspapers. Because of time pressures, only three national figures associated with these disputes were interviewed in any detail, but checks on specific points of interpretation and particular events were made with a wider grouping, largely over the phone.

The two principal methods of research employed for the study of ESB were interviews with all the major figures and documentary evidence from files and other sources. Interviews were mainly carried out between January and July of 1993 while Moneypoint Power Station was visited in October 1993 for discussion with two of the figures involved in the change process in the station.

Researching the ESB in the first nine months of 1993 was akin to chasing a moving target. A series of major management appointments were made in May, 1993 to the five new business subdivisions set up following the recommendations of McKinsey Consultants. The values and "high politics" of the Board were themselves undergoing change as the research was being carried out. This provided some unique insights into particular issues and the breakdown of thinking that might have dominated one side of the company or another, particularly generation and distribution. Informal interviews were held with a number of senior Board figures in October 1994 on the second set of McKinsey proposals for downsizing the ESB.

In all, 16 major figures were interviewed in the Board as part of the research. The initial interviews lasted up to two hours and were formal in structure, seeking to establish a baseline of developments and perspectives on the ESB in the previous 20 years, with particular emphasis on developments during the 1980s. Eleven of the interviewees were either at senior executive or Director level in the ESB and they included Board members. Five senior trade union figures were interviewed. Over half the subjects were interviewed a second time and some on a third occasion for corroboration, updating developments and for assistance on matters of interpretation.

A tape recorder was used for the bulk of the interviews. But informal comments at the beginning and particularly the end of discussions were carefully noted. All tapes and notes were fully transcribed onto a separate computer file for ease of access and purposes of cross-checking and linking in with historical material from the files.

A standard six question interview schedule was initially used with all interviewees concentrating on the difficulties within the Board's industrial relations, the impact of the dispute and why internal systems failed to pick up that it was coming. The second part of the interview format concentrated on the outcomes of the dispute in terms of the industrial relations system and the extent to which it had been undermined or faced extinction. The extent to which the 1991 dispute signalled a break with what went before was explored in detail.

Files in the ESB Registry provided a highly documented and voluminous source of material into developments. In particular they provided insights and "snapshots" of management thinking about major industrial relations problems at different stages from both a short-term and long-term perspective. Material from the files proved invaluable in jogging memories and eliciting fresh insights. Internal reports on the new management strategy within generation and how it emerged, and studies linked to the Cassells Committee also proved useful. Overall, the research method had its strengths and weaknesses. Information on crucial key developments, weaknesses or conflicts in strategy were not always easy to elicit on the first outing. The mention of other "embedded" or largely obscured developments by the interviewer brought more information and facts. Subjects waited for the mention of keywords or developments before going into more detail on their implication in the overall picture. In this sense, information and historical perspective came in layers which had to be literally mined. And subjects occasionally cautioned against the publication of obvious conclusions fearing for the overall well-being of the organisation.

Overall, the ESB proved a highly cultured and layered organisation to research. The detail and discussion on the other semi-states in chapters one and two does not claim to be exhaustive, but merely attempts to outline and analyse the key events in a number of companies and their still unfolding momentous implications.

REFERENCES

PRIMARY SOURCES

ESB Documentation
Files held in the ESB File Registry, Lower Fitzwilliam Street, Dublin

Primary Sources published by the Electricity Supply Board, Dublin

1980   *Personnel Policy in the ESB (Fahy)*
1984   *Report on the Organisation Structure, Roles and Relationships (Miller Barry Report)*
1988   *Labour Court Recommendation LCR12165 on ESB*
1990   *Connecting With the Future — ESB Strategies for the 1990s*
1991   *Management of Change in Power Stations — Progress Through People*
1991   *Employee Relations in the ESB — Negotiators Handbook*
1991   *Joint Industrial Council Recommendation 2233B*
1991   *Government Statement on ESB Dispute on 23 April*
1991   *TEEU Statement on ESB Dispute on 22 April*
1992   *Reshaping ESB to Meet the Challenges of the 1990s (McKinsey Report)*
1993   *Employee Relations in the ESB — Negotiators Handbook*
1993   *Final Report of the Joint Steering Committee — Review of Relationships Within ESB (Cassells Report)*

Published by the Labour Court, Dublin
1991   *Labour Court Recommendation LCR13467 on RTE*
1994   *Labour Court Recommendation LCR14506 on Irish Steel*
1994   *Labour Court Recommendation LCR14552 on TEAM Aer Lingus*

Newspapers and Publications
Business and Finance
Irish Independent
Irish Times
Industrial Relations News

GOVERNMENT PUBLICATIONS

(All published by the Government Publications Office, Dublin)

1969   *Final Report of the Committee on Industrial
       Relations in the Electricity Supply Board (Fogarty
       Report)*
1984   *Report of the National Planning Board*
1986   *Joint Oireachtas Report on Semi-State Bodies*
1991   *Programme for Economic and Social Progress*
1991   *Central Statistics Office Quarterly Industrial
       Dispute Figures*
1992   *Report of the Industry Policy Review Group — A
       Time for Change: Industrial Policy for the 1990s
       (Culliton Report)*
1993   *The Response of the Government to the Moriarty
       Task Force on the Implementation of the Culliton
       Report (Moriarty Report)*
1994   *Programme for Competitiveness and Work*

BOOKS AND ARTICLES

Aer Lingus (1993): *Strategy for the Future, The Cahill Rescue Plan
        for Aer Lingus*, Dublin: Aer Lingus
An Post (1991): *An Post Viability Plan*, Dublin: An Post
Batstone, E. (1988): *The Reform of Workplace Industrial
        Relations*, Oxford: Clarendon Press
Beer, M. and Spector, B. (1985): "Corporatewide
        Transformations in Human Resource Management" in R.E.
        Walton and P.R. Lawrence (eds), *HRM — Trends and
        Challenges*, Boston: Harvard Business School Press
Canning, L. (1981): "Public Sector Industrial Relations: The
        Case of the Electricity Supply Board" in H. Pollock (ed.),

The Reform of Industrial Relations, Dublin: The O'Brien Press

Canning, L. (1994): *Address at the SIPTU Seminar*, Dublin: SIPTU

Chubb, B. (1992): *Federation of Irish Employers, 1942-1992*, Dublin: Gill and Macmillan

Clegg, H. (1990): "The Oxford School of Industrial Relations", *Warwick Papers in Industrial Relations*, 31, Coventry: University of Warwick

Cowen, B. (1994): *Address to Dáil Éireann on 4 March on the Programme for Competitiveness and Work*, Dublin: Department of Transport, Energy and Communications

Cradden, T. (1992): "Trade Unionism and HRM: The Incompatibles?", *Journal of Irish Business and Administrative Research*, 13: 37-48

Davy Stockbrokers (1994): *Report on TEAM Aer Lingus*, Dublin: Davy Stockbrokers

Edwards, C. and Heery, E. (1989): *Management Control and Union Power*, Oxford: Clarendon Press

Ferner, A. (1988): *Governments, Managers and Industrial Relations — Public Enterprises and Their Political Environment*, Oxford: Basil Blackwell

Fox, A. (1966): "Industrial Sociology and Industrial Relations", *Royal Commission on Trade Unions and Employers' Associations*, Research Paper 3, London: HMSO

Gillen, P., McGrail, M., O'Donnell, E. and Murphy, P. (1994): *Report of the Board of Assessors on TEAM Aer Lingus on behalf of the ICTU*, Dublin: ICTU

Goldthorpe, J. (1974): "Industrial Relations in Great Britain: A Critique of Reformism", *Politics and Society*, 419-52

Guest, D. (1990): "Human Resource Management and the American Dream", *Journal of Management Studies*, 27: 376-97

Industrial Relations News (IRN) (1994): *Restructuring and Culture Change to Meet Today's Reality — Conference Report*, Dublin: IRN

Kerr, C. (1964): *Labor and Management in Industrial Society*, New York: Anchor Books

Kochan, T., McKersie, R. and Cappelli, P. (1984): "Strategic Choice and Industrial Relations Theory", *Industrial Relations*, 23: 16-39

Kochan, T., Katz, H.C. and McKersie, R. (1986): *The Transformation of American Industrial Relations*, New York: Basic Books

Lawrence, P. (1985): "The History of Human Resource Management in American Industry" in R.E. Walton and P.R. Lawrence (eds), *HRM — Trends and Challenges, Boston*: Harvard Business School Press

Lee, J.J. (1989): *Ireland 1912-1985: Politics and Society*, Cambridge: Cambridge University Press

Manning, M. and McDowell, M. (1984): *A History of the Electricity Supply Board*, Dublin: Gill and Macmillan

McCabe, J. (1993): *Management of Change in a Major ESB Substation*, unpublished M.Sc. (Mgt.) dissertation, Dublin: Trinity College Dublin

Metcalf, D. (1989): "Water Notes Dry Up: The Impact of Donovan Reform Proposals and Thatcherism At Work on Labour Productivity in British Manufacturing Industry", *British Journal of Industrial Relations*, 27: 1-31

Moriarty, P. (1991): *Address to the World Electricity Conference — The Future of the Integrated Utility in a European Context, London*: World Electricity Conference

Pizzorno, A. (1978): "Political Exchange and Collective Identity in Industrial Conflict" in C. Crouch and A. Pizzorno (eds), *The Resurgence of Class Conflict Since 1968*, London: Macmillan Press

Quinn, R. (1994): *Address at the launch of the Institute of Personnel and Development's Annual Programme of Events*, Dublin: Department of Employment and Enterprise

Roche, W.K. and Brannick, T. (1987): "Strikes and the Development of Industrial Relations in the ESB", *Industrial Relations News*, 21: 17-9

Roche, W.K. (1987): *Social Integration, Union Policies and Strategic Power: The Development of Militancy Among Electricity Generating Station Workers in the Republic of Ireland 1950-1982*, unpublished D. Phil thesis, Oxford: University of Oxford

Roche, W.K. (1992): "The Liberal Theory of Industrialism and the Development of Industrial Relations in Ireland" in J.H. Goldthorpe and C. T. Whelan (eds*), The Development of Industrial Society in Ireland*, Oxford: Oxford University Press for the British Academy

Royal Commission on the Trade Unions and Employers' Associations (1968): *Report of the Royal Commission on the Trade Unions and Employers' Associations*, London: HMSO

Simpson Xavier Horwath Consulting (1994): *Irish Steel Limited — Review of Strategy for Viability on behalf of the Minister for Enterprise and Employment*, Dublin: Simpson Xavier Horwath Consulting

Storey, J. (1992): *Developments in the Management of Human Resources,* Oxford: Blackwell Business

Stoy Hayward (1994): *Report to TEAM Aer Lingus*, London: Stoy Hayward

Sweeney, P. (1990): *The Politics of Public Enterprise and Privatization,* Dublin: Tomar

Sweeney, P. (1991): "The Employment Effects of the Commercialisation of Irish Public Enterprise", *Labour Market Review*, 2: 17-25

Walton, R. (1985): "Towards a Strategy of Eliciting Employee Commitment Based on Policies of Mutuality" in R.E. Walton and P.R. Lawrence (eds), *HRM — Trends and Challenges*, Boston: Harvard University Press

Webb, S. and Webb, B. (1897): *Industrial Democracy*, London: Longmans Green & Co.

INDEX